Geneviève Susemihl

# 70 Classic and New Playground Games
## More Movement for Classroom, Camp and Campus

A Blue Baltic Book

# 70 Classic and New Playground Games

## More Movement for Classroom, Camp and Campus

Geneviève Susemihl

A Blue Baltic Book

Bibliografische Information der Deutschen Nationalbibliothek: Die Deutsche Nationalbibliothek verzeichnet diese Publikation in der Deutschen Nationalbibliografie; detaillierte bibliografische Daten sind im Internet über http://dnb.dnb.de abrufbar.



Manufacturing and Publishing:
BoD – Books on Demand, Norderstedt

ISBN: 978-3-7578-9198-5

# Content

# Introduction

The playground is a fantastic place to play. Playground games are great fun. We all remember fondly the days of playing tag, hide and seek or name ball in our childhood. Some of our life's most important lessons are taught outside the classroom and in the social mixing pool of the playground. Indeed, our triumphs at break time may seem insignificant now, but back in the day a hard-won game of rock, paper, scissors or setting a new skipping record may be essential experiences in forming the kind of people we become in adulthood.

A study[1] exploring the school years of Great Britain's grown-ups has revealed the break-time activities they miss most from the playground. The study indicates that former British pupils enjoyed the creative, fun and occasionally hazardous nature of break time play in their childhood. Overall, more than half of them think break time play and playground activities helped to teach them valuable life lessons and to develop team working skills. About forty per cent think it aided the development of their hand-eye coordination, and they also believe that striving on the playground helped to make them more determined and confident in later life.

The results further revealed some firm gender lines between particular activities. Games such as skipping, cat's cradle and hopscotch were far more popular with female students, while marbles, conkers and British Bulldog were the favoured activities for boys. Hide and seek, kiss chase and tag were able to cross gender boundaries and be popular with all kids at break-time. Today, some treasured games and activities that adults recalled have been banned from modern playgrounds, such as British Bulldog, conkers, wrestling and kiss chase because they are considered too physical. Nevertheless, some of these games are introduced in this book as people have been playing them for many generations and they may be interesting in specific English language teaching contexts.

As a quintessential part of childhood, we often think playground games are simply fun but there's so more to them than that. Research[2] has shown that games are essential for children's health and their physical, social, emotional and cognitive development. Playground games offer children the opportunity to be active, which helps to improve their motor skills, coordination, balance and more. From waiting their turn to sharing play equipment, these games allow children to collaborate and develop bonds with others, which is beneficial for helping them to form new

---

[1] The study was commissioned by Casumo.com and the results published by Grant Bailey, "Brits reveal the top 30 playground games from their childhoods", *Mirror*, 26 April 2018, www.mirror.co.uk/news/uk-news/brits-reveal-top-30-playground-12432502.

[2] See for example, Ed Baines and Peter Blatchford (2010), "Children's Games and Playground Activities in School and Their Role in Development," in: Peter Nathan and Anthony D. Pellegrini (Eds.), *The Oxford Handbook of the Development of Play*. New York: Oxford University Press, 261-283.

relationships. Likewise, games teach children how to understand and manage their emotions, which gives them more confidence in spending time with others and helps them taking some risks. Moreover, through experimenting with trial and error, playground activities help children to strengthen their problem solving and thinking skills. These are the skills that help them plan, prioritize, troubleshoot, negotiate and multitask and that are crucial for their success in later life.

Many playground games are organized and goal orientated so they are considered a form of structured play. This type of play is especially beneficial for older children, as they support the development of active listening and problem-solving skills and provide a platform for social interaction that flows through to the way children play together in unstructured play. Besides enjoying and appreciating nature when playing outside, outdoor play is also vitally important for a child's development by helping to improve their immune systems, providing sunshine for vitamin D production and getting a daily dose of fresh air.

Finally, playground games can be very useful while learning English and may help in making the teaching-learning process more effective. Since brain research shows that active kids learn better at school, a game of tag at recess can help kids absorb lessons later in the classroom. Games also provide language practice in all the four skills, namely, reading, speaking, listening and writing. In the EFL classroom, they are of immense values. As a form of Total Physical Response (TPR), a method of teaching language or vocabulary concepts by using physical movement to react to verbal input, they are being successfully applied by many teachers.[3]

This book introduces 70 classic and new playground games and other activities – from ball games, games of tag, circle and memory games to singing and skipping games, scavenger hunts, races and riddles. Most of these games are classic British playground games, but some are favourite games of children in Germany. While some games are best played with young learners, other games are better suited for older players. Many games are favourite activities at camps and even colleges. The instructions are easy to follow and the rules are kept simple. Best of all: Everyone can play – the more players, the better.

So, let's go outside and play.

---

[3] For more information about the Total Physical Response method see The Teacher Toolkit at www.the-teachertoolkit.com/index.php/tool/total-physical-response-tpr.

# 1. Eeny, Meeny, Miny, Moe: Counting-Out Games

A counting-out game or counting-out rhyme is a simple method of 'randomly' selecting a person from a group to be 'it', often for the purpose of playing another game. It usually involves one person pointing at each participant in a circle of players while reciting a rhyme. A new person is pointed at as each word is said. The player who is selected at the conclusion of the rhyme is 'it' or 'out'.

Many counting-out rhymes date back to the 18th century. The historian Henry C. Bolton suggested in his 1888 book *Counting Out Rhymes of Children* that the custom of counting out originated in the "superstitious practices of divination by lots."

Counting rhymes, just like nursery rhymes, are important for language development and cognitive, physical, social and emotional development. Children learn through repetition, and singing rhymes throughout the day helps them to become familiar with numbers and patterns. They hear the sounds vowels and consonants make and learn how to put them together to make words. They practice pitch, volume, voice inflection and the rhythm of language. They also hear new words and are introduced to alliteration, onomatopoeia and imaginative imagery.

The rhymes are short, easy to repeat and funny and allow children to develop a sense of humour. The rhymes use patterns, sequences, numbers and counting, and children learn recall, memorization and simple math skills as they recite them. Besides, they develop their mouth and tongue muscles by using the different sounds, and rhymes that involve movement help with coordination. Sharing the rhymes provides a safe and secure bond between the children, and positive physical touch between them is important for social development.

Keeping all that in mind, let's start counting: "Ip dip, dog shit, you are (not) it."

Ip dip doo,
the dog's got the flu,
the cat's got chicken pox,
out goes you.

Eeny, meeny, miny, moe,
catch a tiger by the toe,
if he hollers, let him go,
eeny, meeny, miny, moe.

Inky binky bonky,
daddy had a donkey,
donkey died, daddy cried,
inky binky bonky.

Cindereller, dressed in yeller,
went upstairs to kiss her feller.
Made a mistake and kissed a snake,
came downstairs with a bellyache.
How many doctors did it take?
1, 2, 3, 4, 5, 6, 7, 8!
(Whoever is #8 is it.)

My mother and your mother were
washing clothes,
my mother punched your mother
right in the nose.
What colour was her blood?
(The colour chosen is spelled out.)
(Whoever gets the last letter is 'it'.)

Ink-a-dink-a-do,
a bottle of ink,
cork fell out and you stink.
My mother told me to pick
the very best one and you are not it.

Ip dip, cow shit
hanging on the line,
wind blew, shit flew,
out pops you.

Tinker, tailor,
soldier, sailor,
rich man, poor man,
beggar man, thief.

Bubble gum, bubble gum,
in a dish,
how many pieces
do you wish?

Engine, engine #9,
going down Chicago line.
If the train falls off the track,
do you want your money back?
(The person picked says yes or no.)
(The 'counter' spells Y-E-S – or N-O.)
And you are it!

Daisy, daisy, who shall it be?
Who shall it be who will marry me?
Rich man, poor man, beggar man, thief,
doctor, lawyer, merchant, chief,
tinker, tailor, soldier, sailor.
[X] horses in a stable,
one jumps out.
(In place of [X], the number of players is
used, changing as they are taken out.)

## 2. Throwing and Tossing: Ball Games

In 2009, the ball was inducted into the US National Toy Hall of Fame. But it's role in childhood play stretches back to the beginnings of civilization. In fact, the ball is considered one of the earliest children's toys. In ancient Egypt children played games with balls made from papyrus or leather with straw stuffing, and ancient Roman children played ball games such as dodge-ball and catch, using balls made from reeds and linen or inflated pigs' bladders.

Ball games are heaps of fun. They can be used in many different ways and provide multiple benefits across many areas of development, including hand-eye coordination, gross and fine motor skills, spatial awareness, grasping skills, balance and timing. Through ball play children learn patience, turn-taking and sportsmanship, and by interacting, communicating, cooperating and helping each other, they are learning many more social and emotional skills.

Likewise, learning how to play a variety of ball games is an ideal way to keep children fit. From soccer to tennis and netball, children can run for miles without even noticing because their mind is focused on the action and not the physical exertion. Long hours of energetic ball play will wear them out and improves their sleep quality, which helps them function better in every aspect of their lives.

There are countless different ball games played at schoolyards and camps throughout the world, a few of which are introduced on the next pages.

# Four-Square

| | |
|---|---|
| About the game: | A great recess game, also called down ball or box ball. |
| In the classroom: | In a variation, children can practice their vocabulary. |

| | |
|---|---|
| Number of players: | 10-20 |
| Equipment: | a ball |
| Duration: | 10 minutes |
| Preparation: | none |

*How to play:*

Four Square is played on a hard-surfaced square court that measures between three and nine meters on each side and is divided into four identical boxes creating four squares of equal size labelled 1 to 4 or A to D.

One player occupies each of the four squares at a time; the other players wait in line. Square number 4 is the highest-ranked square, and therefore the server's square. Play starts with the server throwing the ball into another square. It must bounce in the square. The player who's square it lands in volleys the ball into another square. Play continues with players volleying the ball into each other's squares until someone is out.

A player is out if the ball does not land inside a square, the player does not volley the ball before the second bounce, or a player hits the ball out of turn. It is not allowed to carry, catch or hold the ball during play. A ball that lands on the line is IN. No one can be out on the serve.

Each time a player gets out, that player leaves the court and enters the back of the line. The remaining players move to the higher numbered square. Square number 1 is then filled by a new player from the line of awaiting players. The goal of the game is to move up to the servers' square. Each round, one point is awarded to the person in square 4 (the server); winner of the game is the first player to has got the most points when the game ends.

*Variations:*

In the English classroom, you can play *Alphabet Soup*. With each hit, players say a word in alphabetical order, e.g., apple, butter, cinema, door, egg, fridge, etc.

*Did you know?*

Every year, the Four-Square World Championships takes place in Bridgton, Maine. In 2012, a group of seventeen Needham High School students and alumni broke the previous world record by playing for 34 hours.

# Hit the Stick

| | |
|---|---|
| About the game: | It is also called Hit the Coin. |
| In the classroom: | A careful aim and a light touch are the required skills. |

| | |
|---|---|
| Number of players: | 2 |
| Equipment: | a ball as well as a coin or an ice cream stick |
| Duration: | 10 minutes |
| Preparation: | none |

*How to play:*

The game is played by two players on a level two-square stretch of the sidewalk. The players stand at either end of two concrete squares with a coin or stick placed directly in the centre seam. The object is to hit the coin or stick with the ball and, even better, attempt to flip it over. Each hit brings one point, each flip is worth two, with play ending once a player reaches 11 or 21.

If there are more people who want to play, they form a waiting line. If a player steps over the line of his square, he is out and the next player in the waiting line comes in.

Some find Hit the Stick more appealing because it's more of a kick to see the stick flip up and turn in the air than checking to see if the penny or nickel is heads or tails. Historically, some would play with the winner buying ice cream.

*Variations:*

The basic laws of physics add an interesting twist to this game. Often when the target is hit, it jumps towards the other player. This can present the nearer player an advantage as he can now lean forward and softly drop the ball on the stick. A soft touch tends to keep the stick from jumping away, thereby allowing a player to easily rack up points. On the other hand, the other player has a longer, more difficult throw, even though he may have hit the stick/coin first.

# Hot Potato

| | |
|---|---|
| About the game: | Hot Potato is a favourite playground game in England. |
| In the classroom: | Children love the excitement of counting backwards. |

| | |
|---|---|
| Number of players: | 10-20 |
| Equipment: | a ball |
| Duration: | 10 minutes |
| Preparation: | none |

*How to play:*

Players form a circle and pass the ball around the circle from player to player, quite slowly at first. One person calls out "Hot Potato" and counts from ten to one. The ball becomes a 'hot potato' that no one wants to hold and gets passed faster and faster.

The person who is left holding the ball on 'one' goes down on one knee. A player who is left holding the 'hot potato' a second time must go down on two knees. If a player catches the 'hot potato' a third time, he is out. As the game goes on, he will be joined by more and more players, until eventually there will be just two players left in the game.

In the final round the ball is passed back and forth between them until one of the players who is out calls "hot potato" and counts down from ten to one. The last person left with the 'hot potato' on the counted one loses. The other player wins.

*Variations:*

When played with a large group of players, they can be out of the game at the first time when holding the ball on 'one'.

# Name Ball

| | |
|---|---|
| About the game: | A great game to help learn each other's names. |
| In the classroom: | Practice vocabulary, such as colours, fruits or animals. |

| | |
|---|---|
| Number of players: | 10-20 |
| Equipment: | a ball (tennis ball or Koosh ball) |
| Duration: | 10 minutes |
| Preparation: | none |

*How to play:*

To start, players stand in a circle and pass the ball around. Each player who has the ball should say his or her name. Once the ball has gone around the circle, change direction and send the ball all the way back. Now everyone has heard everyone else's name twice.

Then start throwing the ball to someone across the circle. It should be thrown so it is easy to catch. Each person says his or her own name and then the name of the person to whom he or she is throwing the ball. If anyone forgets the person's name, it's okay to ask. It will go something like this: John has got the ball.

> John: "John ... Katie" (John throws the ball to Katie).
> Katie: "Katie ... Sarah" (Katie throws the ball to Sarah).

Later, members of the group only say the name of the person to whom they are throwing the ball. It is okay to ask for a name if anyone forgets.

After a while, the group can no longer ask for names. If a mistake is made, such as hesitating, forgetting a name, getting it wrong, throwing badly or missing the ball, that person must go down on one knee. The second mistake means they put one arm behind their back. The third mistake means they must close one eye. With the fourth mistake, they are out and move out of the circle. You might need to nominate a referee for the final stage to avoid arguments. The last players left in the circle are the winners, but really everyone wins because after playing this game you will all know each other's names.

*Variations:*

Add a second and third ball so more than one ball is being thrown at a time. Or rearrange the circle and have the players stand somewhere different in the circle but continue to toss the ball in the same order.

You can also give the players each a name of a colour, a fruit, a vegetable or an animal. They have to remember the words and practice them.

# Queenie, Queenie

About the game:           This is a common children's playground game.
In the classroom:           Children learn a funny verse and practice their English.

Number of players:         5-15
Equipment:               a ball
Duration:                10 minutes
Preparation:            none

*How to play:*

A person is picked to be the 'queenie', and that person turns her back to everyone else. The 'queenie' then throws the ball over her shoulder and one of the other players needs to catch it or pick it up. Everyone, except the 'queenie', puts their hands behind their backs so that the 'queenie' doesn't know who has the ball. The 'queenie' then turns around and everyone shouts:

> "Queenie, Queenie who's got the ball?
> Are they short, or are they tall?
> Are they hairy, or are they bald?
> You don't know because you don't have the ball!"
>
> "Queenie, Queenie who's got the ball?
> See I haven't got it,
> It isn't in my pocket,
> Queenie, Queenie who's got the ball?"

The 'queenie' must guess who has the ball through a process of elimination. If the player with the ball is the last one to be picked, that player becomes the new 'queenie'.

*Variations:*

To make it more difficult for 'queenie' to guess who has the ball, the players all keep their left hand behind their back and show the right hand, then put the right hand behind and show the left hand as they say the chant. They keep on swapping hands. The person with the ball must keep swapping the ball behind their back from left to right hands and must make sure they don't drop it.

# 3. Catch Me If You Can: Games of Tag

Tag is fun! At all times and in all cultures and societies, children have been playing tag. These days, however, there are many different versions of the game. Some incorporate beloved characters from movies and others encourage kids to act like animals or robots. Some tag games are best played in P.E. class since you will need cones, mats or bean bags, and others are perfect to play with friends.

Tag is a playground game involving one or more players chasing other players in an attempt to 'tag' and mark them out of play, usually by touching with a hand. There are many variations; most forms have no teams, scores or equipment. Usually, when a person is tagged, the tagger says, "Tag, you're 'it'!" The last one tagged is 'it' for the next round. Many variants modify the rules for team play or place restrictions on tagged players' behaviour. A simple variation makes tag an elimination game, so that tagged players drop out of play. Other variations include base and truce terms. Players may be safe from being tagged under certain circumstances, for example if they are within a pre-determined area or when touching a particular structure.

Tag is a great game for building physical literacy in children. In fact, a game of tag helps kids learn fundamental movement and sports skills that can encourage them to stay active for life. Tag works for a variety of ages and abilities and can be easily modified depending on where you are. Savvy players can add new rules, strategize ways for not getting tagged and vary the mechanisms for getting freed.

Ready to play? Choose one of the tag games from this chapter and start running!

# It/Tag and 18 Variations

About the game:          Games of tag are most common on the playground.
In the classroom:        A great game for an active learning break.

Number of players:       2 or more
Equipment:               none
Duration:                no limit
Preparation:             none

## How to play:

Players decide who is going to be 'it', often using a counting-out game. The player selected to be 'it' then chases the others, attempting to tag one of them (by touching them with a hand) as the others try to avoid being tagged. A tag makes the tagged player 'it'. In some variations, the previous 'it' is no longer 'it' and the game can continue indefinitely; in other variations, both players remain 'it' and the game ends when all players have become 'it'. Here are 18 variations of the game:

## Ants and Frogs

Choose a few children to be frogs, the rest of the children are ants. Determine a home base for the ants and a starting point for the frogs. At the signal, the frogs move around trying to tag the ants. When a player gets tagged, they must sit down on the ground. At this point, the ants that have not been tagged can try to 'save' their fellow ants by getting four ants form a circle around the tagged ant and lead them to the home base. When all four ants are walking with the tagged ant in the middle of them, they cannot be tagged. After the ants reach home base, all five ants have two seconds to get away before they can be tagged by the frogs. The game is over when all the ants have been tagged and sitting down.

## Blind Man's Bluff

One player, designated as 'it', is blindfolded and gropes around attempting to tag the other players without being able to see them, while the other players scatter and try to avoid the person who is 'it', hiding in plain sight and sometimes teasing the 'it' to influence 'it' to change direction. When the 'it' player catches someone, the caught player becomes 'it'. *Variation:* Whenever any player is tagged by 'it', that player is out of the game. The game proceeds until all players are out of the game, at which point another round of the game starts, with either the first player or the last player to be tagged becoming the next 'it' player.

*Chain Tag*

One player is 'it' and attempts to tag other players. Each tagged player becomes 'it' as well, with all the 'it' players required to form and remain in a human chain by holding hands. Only the two players at either end of the chain can tag other players. The game ends once all players have been tagged, with the last person tagged being the winner. *Variation:* Once there are four people on the chain, they can break into two groups of two. The last person unattached is the winner.

*Elbow Tag*

At the start of the game, two of the players become a cat and mouse respectively, with all other players becoming pitchers. All pitchers pair off and form a circle around the perimeter of the playing field, with each pair holding each other by the elbow. The cat's goal is to tag the mouse; if the mouse links their elbow with one of the pitchers, then the pitcher who is not connected to the mouse disconnects from the pairing and swaps roles with the mouse. If the cat catches the mouse, then they swap roles.

*Flashlight Tag*

Flashlight tag is played at night. Rather than physically tagging, the 'it' player tags by shining a flashlight beam on other players.

*Freeze Tag*

A player is deemed 'it'. When a person is tagged by 'it', they are 'frozen' (staying still in the place where they were tagged). All 'unfrozen' players can then touch frozen players to 'unfreeze' them, allowing them to be back in play. The game ends when 'it' freezes all but one of the players who is then 'it' during the next game. In a variation, there may be multiple players who are 'it' working together.

*Kick the Can*

A can is placed in an open space. The other players run off and hide, while the 'it' player tries to find and tag them. Tagged players are sent to jail. Any player who has not been caught can kick the can, setting the other players free from jail.

*Memory Tag*

All players are taggers. If a player is tagged the player must bob down where they were tagged, but remember who it was that tagged them. When the person that tagged them gets tagged, they can stand up and continue the game.  Rock, paper, scissors is a great way to settle any disputes.

### Rescue Tag or Stuck in the Mud

A group of children are running around on a field, and one person is 'it'. When tagged, players become 'stuck in the mud'. They cannot move and must stand with their legs apart. The only way to be rescued is for a non-tagged player to crawl through their legs. Players are safe while crawling under legs and cannot be tagged. The game ends when all players have been tagged.

### Sock Tag

A sock is filled with a small amount of flour in the toe of the sock; the sock is then gripped by the leg hole and wielded as a flail. Striking a player with any part of the sock counts as a tag. When the sock strikes the player, the impact releases enough flour to leave a mark which serves as proof that the player was tagged.

### Capture the Flag

The field is divided into two halves, one for each team, and the goal of each team is to have its players go into enemy territory, grab the 'flag' located in the back of their territory, and then make it back to friendly territory without being tagged.

### Fox and Geese

The fox starts at the centre of a spoked wheel, and the geese flee from the fox along the spokes and around the wheel. Geese that are tagged become foxes. The intersections of the spokes with the wheel are safe zones.

### Hens – Vipers – Foxes

There are three teams in this game: the hens, the vipers and the foxes, with each team having its own designated area ('camp'). Each team can tag players of one of the other teams (i.e., hens can tag vipers, vipers tag foxes, and foxes tag hens) to imprison them within the tagging team's camp, with the prisoners only being able to be freed by a tag from the third team.

### Merchants and Pirates

Two players are selected to be the pirates, the rest of the players are merchants. Both groups start at opposing ends of the playing field. After the starting signal, both groups run from their end of the playing field to the other. The pirates must try and tag the merchants. To tag them, they must grab a player and move him to the pirate's side of the playing field. All merchants tagged this way become pirates in the next round. Then, a new round starts, and again the merchants try to reach to other end of the playing field without being captured by the pirates. The last (two) remaining merchants start a new game as new pirates. Ensure to define a level of 'force' that may be applied by the pirates to capture (and by the merchants to defend). Nobody should get hurt during the game, so, obviously, biting, hitting and other forms of excessive force are not permitted.

### Polar Bear and Penguin

The players are standing in a circle, always two players behind each other. Two players are chosen to be the polar bear and the penguin. The polar bear tries to tag the penguin. When successful, they switch roles and again try to catch each other. The penguin can try to escape by standing in front of one of the pairs in the circle. Then, the rear player in this pair becomes the new polar bear, while the previous polar bear is transformed to the new penguin.

### Prisoner's Base

In prisoner's base, each team starts in a chain, holding hands, with one end of the chain touching the base. The two end players on each team break from the chain and try to tag each other, taking them to their base if they do. The end pair progressively break from the chain and join the tagging. As with Cops and Robbers, prisoners can be freed by tagging them in the base.

### Manhunt

Manhunt is a mixture of hide and seek and tag, often played during the night. One person is 'it', while the other players must hide. The person who is 'it' tries to find and tag them. The game is over when all players are out. *Variation:* Manhunt is sometimes played in teams. In one variant, there is a home base in which players are safe; the game ends when all players who are not safe are out. In another variant, flashlights are used.

### Steal the Bacon

There are two teams on opposite ends of the field, with an object placed in the centre of the field. Once play begins, one player from each team attempts to grab the object and then run back to their own team's end of the field to score a point. If a player is holding the object and is tagged by an opponent, then they fail and the other team scores a point.

# British Bulldog or Red Rover

| | |
|---|---|
| About the game: | A British schoolyards game, popular in many countries. |
| In the classroom: | Players develop many skills and agility. |

| | |
|---|---|
| Number of players: | 10-20 |
| Equipment: | none |
| Duration: | 10 minutes |
| Preparation: | none |

*How to play:*

The aim of the game is to run from one end of the playing field to the other, without being caught by the bulldogs. Designate a playing area with clear boundaries. This game can be played in any large open space, indoors or outdoors. The selected location consists of one main playing area, with two 'home' areas on opposing sides (similar to the try-zone areas used in rugby or American football), marked by a line or some other marker.

Choose 1-3 students to start in the middle of the playing field. They are the 'British Bulldogs'. All the other players line up, shoulder to shoulder, at one end of the playing area (home). The game starts when the players in the middle call out, "British Bulldog!" On this signal, all players must run to the other side of the playing area, while trying to avoid being tagged by one of the British Bulldogs. Any player who is tagged becomes a British Bulldog for the next round. The last few players start as the British Bulldogs for the next round.

*Variations:*

In the game Red Rover, a New York chasing game from the 1890s, one person, the 'Red Rover', is chosen as catcher and stands in the middle of the street, while the other players form a line on the pavement on one side. He calls any player he wants by name: "Red Rover, Red Rover, let [player's name] come over!", and that player must then run to the opposite sidewalk. If he is caught as he runs across, he must help the Red Rover to catch the others.

*Did you know?*

British Bulldog is a descendant of traditional chasing games recorded from the 18th and 19th centuries, which partially evolved into collision-sport-related games during the early 20th century. In a sport's historical context, British Bulldog has been used as a skill-and-drill device to reinforce and further develop locomotion skills vital to American football, rugby, soccer, hockey and related team sports.

# Cops and Robbers

| | |
|---|---|
| About the game: | A great game for two contending teams. |
| In the classroom: | A fun game that can be incorporated into a story. |

| | |
|---|---|
| Number of players: | 10-20 |
| Equipment: | 7-9 hula hoops, bean bags and traffic cones |
| Duration: | 20 minutes |
| Preparation: | none |

*How to play:*

Place the hula hoops all over the grounds outdoor or the gym, not too close to-gether, and place the bean bags inside the hoops (2-3 bags in one hoop). Use the traffic cones to mark a safe zone and possibly the jail. Divide the group into two teams of equal size – the team of the cops and the team of the robbers. An extra person joins the robbers. The robbers stand in the middle of the playing area together as a group, while the cops are placed throughout the entire playing area.

The point of the game is for the robbers to run around and not get tagged by the cops who will be chasing them. The robbers have to run and grab as many bean bags as possible, which is considered the 'loot', and bring it back to the home base safely without getting caught by the cops. As long as a robber stands inside a hula hoop he is considered safe and cannot be tagged. But only one robber at a time can stand inside a hula hoop. If a robber makes it to the safe zone with the 'loot', then he drops the bean bag and takes off again to grab more bean bags.

If a cop tags a robber, he is arrested and has to sit down wherever he was tagged or he is taken to the jail. However, if he has a bean bag in hand he must go back and place it in the hula hoop first, then go back and sit down where he was tagged by the cop. The game ends once all the robbers have been caught and are sitting down. If all bean bags are in the safe zone, the robbers win the game. If all of the robbers are sitting down, they have all been arrested and the cops win the game.

*Variations:*

If the game is played as a maze, the cops would count to 15 before beginning the chase. Prisoned robbers can break out of jail if they are touched by a free robber.

*Did you know?*

Janet and Allan Ahlberg's book *Cops and Robbers* is a fun story to accompany the game.

# Dragon's Tail Tag

About the game:                A fun game for any group size.
In the classroom:            To learn tagging skills while performing teamwork.

Number of players:          10-20
Equipment:                  none
Duration:                   10 minutes
Preparation:              none

*How to play:*

Players split into groups of four or more and form chains by linking arms or grabbing each other's waists or shoulders. The last player in each chain carries a scarf, bandanna or long sock to act as a 'tail'. These players tuck the 'tails' into the back of their waist-bands. Each chain is now a 'dragon'.

The game starts by the dragons scattering across a playing area. When the leader of the game shouts "Go!" the dragons chase each other, trying to grab opponents' tails, while protecting their own tails. Only the first player in the dragon chain can grab another team's tail. No sitting on or hiding of tails!

Each team's chain must stay unbroken. Players should decide in advance what the consequences will be if a chain comes loose. For example, the whole team could perform a fitness activity (such as five squats or running a quick lap around the playing area), and/or the chain is required to re-form with a different player at the head and tail.

Play until one player has all the tails, or for a predetermined time period.

*Variations:*

*Sock Tag* or *'Tails' Variation*: Every player gets a tail, and they all play both offense and defence, trying to grab each other's tails while also protecting their own. Instead of players sitting out once their tails have been grabbed, they may perform a fitness activity. When completed, they can re-join the game and try to grab themselves a new tail from another player. Play until one player has all the tails, or for a predetermined time period.

*Giant Dragon Variation*: Another option for a smaller group of players is to make just one dragon. The player at the head of the line tries to steal the tail, while the players in the middle try to stop her without breaking the chain.

# Forty-Forty

| | |
|---|---|
| About the game: | Also known as 123 Home, Bunker 52 or Mob, this game combines elements of 'It' and hide and seek. |
| In the classroom: | A great game during break time. |

| | |
|---|---|
| Number of players: | 10-20 |
| Equipment: | a playing area with various landmarks |
| Duration: | 10 minutes |
| Preparation: | none |

*How to play:*

A player is chosen as 'it' and a landmark such as a tree or lamppost is chosen as the base. Players who are not 'it' run and hide, while the 'it' player counts to a certain number, e.g., to 40 or 100. Then the 'it' player looks for the other players, while the players try to get to base without being seen.

If a player gets to base without being seen, they shout "Forty-forty I'm free", "Forty-forty home", "Forty-forty save myself" or "Forty-forty in" and are then safe, waiting at base for the remainder of the game. In order to catch someone, the 'it' player must see the person, run back, touch the base and say "Forty-forty I see [name]". If the 'seen' player is behind or in an object, it must be specified; e.g. "Forty-forty I see [name] behind that tree" while pointing at it.

Players that are caught by the 'it' player return to base. The last person to be caught by the end of the game is 'it' for the next round. Some variants make the first person caught 'it' for the next round.

*Variations:*

There are variants to allow players to be freed. In some variants, a player reaching base can say "Release, one, two, three" or a similar chant to release one or all captured players. If the last player reaches the base without being spied, they can chant a variant of "Forty-forty, one, two, three, all saved", and all the players are freed to play again.

# Please, Mr. Crocodile

| | |
|---|---|
| About the game: | A fun game for younger players. |
| In the classroom: | Children learn the words for colours and funny rhymes. |

| | |
|---|---|
| Number of players: | 3 and more |
| Equipment: | none |
| Duration: | 10 minutes |
| Preparation: | none |

*How to play:*

All the players – except one who is chosen as 'Mr. Crocodile' – stand side by side at one side of the yard or room, facing the other side. Mr. Crocodile stands in the middle of the yard or room.

The players chant, "Please, Mr. Crocodile, may we cross the river? If not, why not, what's your favourite colour?"

Mr. Crocodile calls out the name of one colour and any of the players wearing that colour are safe to cross past Mr. Crocodile to the other side of the yard/room. For example, if Mr. Crocodile calls, "blue", anyone wearing blue is safe to cross.

Once the safe players are across to the other side of the space, the players not wearing the selected colour must try to run across to the other side of the yard/room without being caught by Mr. Crocodile. The player that is caught becomes the next Mr. Crocodile and the game starts again.

Alternatively, the children may say:

"Please, Mr. Crocodile, may I cross the water to see my baby daughter who lives in a cup and saucer?"

Mr. Crocodile replies with something like "Only if you are wearing something blue."

"Please Mr Crocodile, may we cross the water to see your lovely daughter floating on the water like a cup and saucer?"

Mr Crocodile replies: "Yes, if you're dressed in..."

# Streets and Alleys

| | |
|---|---|
| About the game: | A great schoolyard game for older players. |
| In the classroom: | A fun activity for a PE lesson or any break time. |

| | |
|---|---|
| Number of players: | 10-20 |
| Equipment: | none |
| Duration: | 10-15 minutes |
| Preparation: | none |

*How to play:*

The game is set up by selecting a player to be the cat and another player to be the mouse. One player may be selected to be the caller.

All other players form an equal number of rows and columns. You may have five columns of players with five players in each column, thereby making five rows of players. They should stand close enough together that they can join hands with the other players in their row, and they should also be able to reach the hands with the other players in their column.

Players form a 'street' when they join hands with the players in their column; they form 'alleys' when they join hands with the players in their row. They need to rotate 90 degrees to switch from alleys to streets. Have the players practice switching from streets to alleys and back several times before starting the game.

The cat and the mouse start at opposite ends of the playing area. On the signal, the cat will attempt to catch the mouse (power walking in small spaces). The cat and mouse can only travel on the open streets or alleys; they may not go through, under or over joined hands. While the cat is trying to catch the mouse, the signal caller will call out changes from streets to alleys, or alleys to streets. This helps keep everyone involved in the game, changes the playing field, and can give either the cat or the mouse an advantage or disadvantage.

When the mouse is caught, switch cat and mouse, or have the cat become the mouse and bring in a new cat.

This game can be adapted to several kinds of tag games, especially if the players are having trouble controlling their power walk. If the cat and mouse have trouble controlling their walk, they can balance something on their head or hands, such as erasers, coins or foam patties.

# Ugly Old Witch, What's for Dinner Tonight?

About the game:           A typical English playground game.
In the classroom:        Children practice their food vocabulary.

Number of players:     10-20
Equipment:             none
Duration:              10-15 minutes
Preparation:         none

*How to play:*

One player is the 'witch' and stands at one side of the playing field. The other players stand in a line on the other side. The children call: "Ugly old witch, what's for dinner tonight?"

The witch names some food, choosing long words or phrases with many syllables, such as pizza and fruit salad, spaghetti and tomato sauce, chicken sandwich, fish and chips, rice and red cabbage, potatoes and peas, or Chinese noodle soup.

The children step forward, repeating the words – one step for each syllabus (e.g., chicken sandwich – 4 steps), and call again.

When the children are close to the witch, she calls "little children" and tries to catch as many children as she can, who will then help her and stand on her side.

It is played as long as only one child is left who will be the new witch.

# What's the Time, Mr. Wolf?

About the game:         A classic English game for players of all ages.
In the classroom:         Children practice their counting skills and the time.

Number of players:     10-20
Equipment:           none
Duration:            10 minutes
Preparation:         none

*How to play:*

One player is chosen to be Mr. Wolf and stands facing away from the other players at one end of the playing field. All other players stand in a line at the other end. The players call out, "What's the time, Mr. Wolf?" To this, Mr. Wolf turns and answers with a time – usually an hour ending in "o'clock", for example, "It's 5 o'clock." He then turns his back again while the other players advance with that many steps, counting them aloud as they go ("One, two, three, four, five.").

Then they ask the question again, "What's the time, Mr Wolf?", to which Mr. Wolf continues to respond until the players come very close.

Once the line of players is close to Mr. Wolf, he can respond to the chant with "It's dinner time!", at which point he will chase the players back to the starting line with the aim to catch one of them, who will then become Mr. Wolf for the next round of the game.

It is not uncommon for 'Mr. Wolf' to be allowed to look around at the other players, before answering the question, especially if there is a rule involving penalties applied to 'Mr. Wolf' if a player reaches 'Mr. Wolf' before 'dinner time' is called.

*Variations:*

In some parts of North America, the game is called "What's the Time, Mr. Shark?" when played at a pool, lake or beach. When "lunch time" is called, the players may try running through the water or swimming to get away from the shark.

*Did you know?*

Use the book *What's the Time, Mr. Wolf?* (illustrated by Annie Kubler) to introduce the time with a story.

# Zombie Tag or Humans vs. Zombies

| | |
|---|---|
| About the game: | A survival game of tag played by players of all ages. |
| In the classroom: | A fun activity for a PE lesson or any break time. |

| | |
|---|---|
| Number of players: | at least 10 |
| Equipment: | none |
| Duration: | any duration |
| Preparation: | none |

*How to play:*

This is a survival game of tag, where 'human' players fight off increasingly large numbers of 'zombies'. The goal of the zombies is to turn all the humans into zombies; the humans, meanwhile, must outlast the zombies. If a human is 'turned' (i.e., tagged), then that player becomes a zombie in turn.

At the game's beginning, there are only one or two zombies; the zombies multiply by tagging humans, turning them into zombies. Humans can defend themselves from zombies by using socks, marshmallows, Nerf Blasters or any other toys deemed safe and appropriate. If a zombie is hit by one of these methods of defence, they are stunned (not allowed to interact with the game in any way) for fifteen seconds.

*Did you know?*

Humans vs. Zombies (also called HvZ for short) was created as a live-action game by seven students of Goucher College, Maryland, in 2005, who have since created an official website with general guideline rules and information for other universities to create and customize their own HvZ game. Since then, the game has been played at over 1,000 locations, spanning across six continents. It is played by hundreds of people on campus every semester. Each player signs up and receives a bandanna, which they wear on the upper arm to denote themselves as human. Zombies, who wear their bandanna on the head, tag humans to increase the zombie population. However, following the Virginia Tech shootings in 2007, the game was banned at some colleges.

# 4. Round and Round It Goes: Circle Games

Circle games are a popular activity in any group gathering, be it in classrooms, at camps, family meetings or with fellow students and friends – and for a good reason! They are a great opportunity to bring the group together and there are suitable games for all levels and ages.

Circle games are any games or activities that involve the whole group, sitting in a circle, and are an excellent way to encourage the whole class or group to work together. These games are easy to monitor, ensure that players are on equal ground, and enable everyone to see and hear one another.

Circle games are easy to organize and set up in a hurry, as most of them don't require much preparation or material. They are, therefore, great for filling in gaps and teachers or camp counsellors can get a game going without a lot of effort.

Circle games are also educational. This structured activity allows players to practice and apply social skills, follow certain rules and routines and develop a sense of community. They also allows educators to assess each player's needs and interests, and a lot of language can be generated. In the classroom, circle games can be used as 'warmers' at the beginning of a class or as a 'filler' at the end, or they can be incorporated into the regular routine of a class.

Here is a selection of some favourite circle games that can be used in young learner, youth and adult classes, at camps and at any other occasion.

# Alibi Game

| | |
|---|---|
| About the game: | A fun game for storytelling and attentive listening. |
| In the classroom: | A great way to practise narrative tenses and questions. |

| | |
|---|---|
| Number of players: | 10-20 |
| Equipment: | none |
| Duration: | 10 minutes |
| Preparation: | none |

*How to play:*

Players sit in a circle. One player is chosen to be the detective, and leaves the circle briefly. Another player is chosen as the criminal, without the detective knowing who. The detective returns and stands in the center of the circle. The detective goes around the circle one at a time, asking each person, "Where were you last night?" Each person has to respond with their alibi. They might say: "I was walking my dog, I was at the grocery store, I was watching a movie, etc."

After each person has given their alibi, the detective goes around the circle a second time asking the same question. Everyone but the person who was chosen as the criminal gives the same answer as the first time, but the criminal gives a different alibi. The detective has to remember everyone's alibis from the first time around the circle in order to figure out who is the criminal. If they do not guess correctly, the criminal wins and becomes the next detective.

*Variations:*

When played in the EFL classroom, they players might be given a specific 'story'. Robbers might have robbed a bank, but tell the police that they went to the cinema. Split the class into three groups and give them a letter – A, B and C. All 'A's are criminals. They have been arrested by the police as suspects for a crime and in five minutes they are going to be questioned. Now they need to work together to create a perfect alibi that will prove that they couldn't have robbed the bank. Give them five minutes to prepare their alibis.

The 'B' and 'C' students form teams. They have five minutes to discuss what questions they'll ask; they can take notes. After five minutes bring the 'A's back and put them with pairs of detectives. Suspects must be interviewed separately for the game to work. Detectives have five minutes to ask questions and note down the answers. After five minutes they'll compare their answers in their groups and if they can find two differences in the alibis, the suspects are found guilty.

# Copycat or Follow the Leader

| | |
|---|---|
| About the game: | A fun game of guessing and imitating. |
| In the classroom: | Serves as a good energizer or warm-up activity. |

| | |
|---|---|
| Number of players: | 8-20 |
| Equipment: | none |
| Duration: | 10 minutes |
| Preparation: | none |

*How to play:*

The group sits in a circle. First, they pick one player to be the guesser. That player must leave the room or move away from the circle so they cannot see or hear who is picked to be the leader. Another player is chosen to be the leader for this round. Then the guesser comes back to stand in the middle of the circle.

The leader starts actions that the group must copy, such as clapping, pulling faces, finger-clicking, tummy-rubbing, patting parts of the body, foot-stomping, singing, jumping or a dance move. Everyone in the circle should copy what the leader does at all times. The leader must try to switch the action without being noticed by the guesser.

The guesser observes the circle's actions and has to work out the identity of the leader. It'll be their job to guess who's starting the actions that everyone else is copying. The guesser has three chances to identify the leader. If they guess right, they win the round. Otherwise, the leader wins.

Choose another guesser and leader and start another round.

# Duck, Duck, Goose

| | |
|---|---|
| About the game: | A traditional children's game in England. |
| In the classroom: | An easy game for young players. |

| | |
|---|---|
| Number of players: | 10-20 |
| Equipment: | none |
| Duration: | 10 minutes |
| Preparation: | none |

*How to play:*

A group of players sit in a circle, facing inward, while one player, the 'picker' or 'fox' ('it'), walks around tapping or pointing to each player in turn, calling each a 'duck' until finally calling one a 'goose'.

The 'goose' then quickly rises and chases and tries to tag the 'picker', while the 'picker' tries to return to and sit where the 'goose' had been sitting before. If the picker succeeds, the 'goose' is now the new 'picker', and the process begins again. If the 'goose' succeeds in tagging the 'picker', the 'goose' returns to sit in the previous spot and the 'picker' restarts the process.

With older players, the 'goose' may attempt to tackle the 'picker'.

*Variations:*

*Drop Handkerchief* or *Kiss in the Ring*: The picker touches the shoulder of each person in the ring with a handkerchief saying, "not you", "not you", until the picker reaches the desired chaser, places the handkerchief on the person's shoulder (or behind his back), and says "but you". The picker then runs around the outside of the circle pursued by the chaser. Once the chaser catches the picker, the chaser is entitled to lead the picker into the centre of the ring (and claim a kiss). The original picker then takes the chaser's place in the ring and the chaser becomes the picker for the next round.

*Drip, Drip, Drop*: One player who is 'it' goes around the circle with a container of water and 'drips' a small amount on each person's head. He will then select someone in the circle to 'drop' the entire container on top of them. This player will then try to tag the 'it' before the 'it' sits in the spot of the person who got 'dropped' on. If the 'it' player is tagged, then he will remain 'it' for another round.

# Follow me – Run Away

| | |
|---|---|
| About the game: | German kids know the game as *Komm mit, lauf weg.* |
| In the classroom: | Another fun game for young players. |

| | |
|---|---|
| Number of players: | 10-20 |
| Equipment: | none |
| Duration: | 10 minutes |
| Preparation: | none |

*How to play:*

The players form a big circle. The 'it' player goes around the circle, taps someone and says either "come with me" or "run away".

When the 'it' player says "Come with me!", both players run one lap around the circle; whoever reaches the previously created gap first gets to stop there. The person who did not arrive in time continues to walk in circles and then taps someone else. In "Run Away!", the players run around the circle in opposite directions and try to reach the empty space.

*Variations:*

The game can also be made a little more action-packed. For this version you need at least 16 players who sit on the ground in a star shape, like the spokes of a wheel. The 'it' player walks around the spokes, taps someone sitting at the end of a row and says either "Come with me!" or "Run away!" Now the whole line starts moving and runs around the circle – either in the same direction with the 'it' player, or in the opposite direction. Everyone is trying to get a place in the new series. Whoever arrives last becomes the new 'it'; that player is always allowed to use the indoor lane when running.

# Four on the Couch

About the game:          A fun game for teenagers.
In the classroom:       Memory and thinking are important parts of this game.

Number of players:     at least 12
Equipment:          slips of paper, pens, one 'couch' that seats four people
Duration:           15-20 minutes
Preparation:        write names of players on slips of paper

*How to play:*

First, designate one four-seater couch (or bench, set of chairs or place on a blanket if played on the ground) as the 'couch'. The point of the game is to have all four seats on the 'couch' occupied by your team members. Divide the group into two equal teams and have everyone sit in the circle in the order Team A – Team B – Team A – Team B. Each team has got two players on the 'couch'. One seat stays empty, so you need one more seat than there are people. Then have everyone write their first name down, toss all slips of paper in a hat, and hand them out to everyone again. Each player will get someone else's name. Someone might get his own name, but that's fine. All players must keep the name a secret.

Now you're ready to play. Let's say Ann, Ben, Clara and David are playing. Ann is sitting on the couch, Ben and Clara are sitting in random seats, and David is sitting in the seat to the right of the empty seat and gets to start. He calls out the name of anyone in the circle, like "Clara". Whoever is holding the slip of paper with Clara's name on it (say it is Ben) gets up and moves to sit in the empty chair next to David. Then Ben and David trade papers, so now David is 'Clara', and Ben is whoever was on David's paper (only David and Ben know). Then the person to the right of Ben's old chair gets to call out a name, and so on. The player to the right of the empty chair calls out a name, and the player holding the piece of paper with that name moves to the empty chair, and then the players switch names.

Now remember that Ann started on the 'couch'? Let's pretend she is holding a slip of paper with Eric's name on it. When someone says "Eric", Ann has to get up and move; one of the 'couch' spaces is now open. Faye, who is sitting to the right of where Ann was sitting, gets the chance to fill the open seat on the 'couch' with one of her team members, as long as she can remember one of the names one of her team members is currently holding.

Both teams are trying to figure out the names of the opposite team's members on the couch so they can call them off, and players try to keep track of everything, but with all the seat- and name-switching it can get complicated. In the end, it's a big moment of triumph for the winning team when they occupy the 'couch'.

# Fruit Salad

| | |
|---|---|
| About the game: | A fun game for younger players. |
| In the classroom: | Players practice the words for different fruits. |

| | |
|---|---|
| Number of players: | 10-20 |
| Equipment: | none |
| Duration: | 10 minutes |
| Preparation: | none |

*How to play:*

All players sit in a circle. Choose four different types of fruit. They should walk around the circle, tap people on the shoulder, and give them a fruit name. They should give the fruit names out in order, so every fourth person will be the same fruit. Check that everyone knows what fruit they are.

Now it's good to have a practice round. Players should call out the name of one of the fruits. Anyone with that fruit name should get up, run around the edge of the circle, and sit down in a different place to where they were before.

Keep calling out fruits, and everyone should keep getting up and running around the edge when their fruit name is called. If "fruit salad" is called, everyone should stand up, run around the edge, and sit in a different space to the one they were in before.

Now, tell everyone you're going to call out two fruits. No-one can move until both fruits have been called out. After the second fruit has been called out, both teams can move. Whichever team of fruits is the first to have all its players sit down in a different seat, gets a point. The team with the most points wins. Remind everyone that they cannot stop someone sitting in a space. Make sure each team can go the same number of times – it might help to write down an order of play.

*Variations:*

Make it competitive – the last person to find a seat could be 'out', then a chair can be removed. You could make up a story, so rather than just saying fruits, you could include them in a story about going shopping, or making and eating a fruit salad. If anyone doesn't run, they could be out. You could call out fruits that aren't in the game. You could speed up or slow down the game. You could also call fruits in pairs. Finally, you could tell the fruits how to move each time they call their name, such as crawling, jumping or tiptoeing.

# Smarties Games

| | |
|---|---|
| About the game: | A great game for getting to know each other. |
| In the classroom: | Players practice talking about themselves. |

| | |
|---|---|
| Number of players: | 10-20 |
| Equipment: | M&M's, Smarties, Gummi Bears or other sweets |
| Duration: | 10 minutes |
| Preparation: | none |

*How to play:*

The players are standing in a circle. Each player takes as many sweets as they consider appropriate and right (while no hints are given what is 'right'), or they take between 2 and 5 pieces.

When each player has taken their share, the actual task is disclosed: For each piece of candy the player has taken, they have to disclose something about themselves. Usually, you offer some guidelines for what information to disclose, like: What's your name? How old are you? What's your hobby? Where do you live? Have you got a brother or sister?

Players then talk about themselves:

> "My name is...
>
> I'm ... years old.
>
> My hobby is ...
>
> I live in ...
>
> I've got a brother and two sisters."

If a player cannot say as many sentences as the number of sweets determine, he or she may listen to the other players and say the sentences later in the round.

# The Orange Game

| | |
|---|---|
| About the game: | It reveals computer science without using computers. |
| In the classroom: | Young players practice words for colours and fruit. |

| | |
|---|---|
| Number of players: | 5 |
| Equipment: | 5 T-shirts in different colours, different fruit in colours matching the T-shirts: 2 green apples, 2 bananas, 2 oranges, 2 red apples, 1 eggplant |
| Duration: | basic challenge 5-10 minutes |
| Preparation: | none |

*How to play:*

The aim of the game is that each person must hold the right coloured two pieces of fruit in their hands, except one who will be holding only one piece of fruit.

Five players are sitting in a circle, each wearing a differently coloured T-shirt (red, orange, blue, green and yellow). At the beginning, the fruit is distributed randomly among them.

Players are only allowed to pass fruit to someone beside them who has an empty hand. A move from player two to four is not allowed, because they are not sitting next to each other. Players may have to give up their own coloured fruit to help the team reach the goal. With some cooperation each player ends up with the right pieces of fruit.

Younger players learning English can say the colours and fruit while passing them, e.g., "I pass a red apple" or "A yellow banana goes to orange".

*Variations:*

You can experiment with different layouts for your network. A straight-line version with five players sitting in a line is not as difficult as it might seem at first.

The basic challenge can be done in 5 or 10 minutes depending on how well the players work together, but exploring variations and different layouts and discussing general strategies could take up to 30 minutes.

# The Puking Kangaroo

| | |
|---|---|
| About the game: | A fun game for concentration. |
| In the classroom: | A great for repeating vocabulary and silly movements. |

| | |
|---|---|
| Number of players: | 7-20 |
| Equipment: | none |
| Duration: | 5 minutes |
| Preparation: | none |

*How to play:*

All players stand in a circle; one stands in the middle. This player points to a person and says, for example, "Puking Kangaroo". This means that the person being pointed at forms a kangaroo pouch with his arms and the two players next to him 'puke' into the pouch (movement suggestion and sound). If one person oversleeps the call or does something wrong, they swap places with the player in the middle and continue giving commands. Start slowly, with three simple figures, and gradually increase the difficulty. Other commands may be:

- ◇ Elephant: Centre makes trunk with arms, sides form the ears with the arms.
- ◇ Mixer: Centre raises arms above neighbour's heads, sides turn like mixers.
- ◇ Toaster: Sides form toaster of arms, centre pops like toast and says "Bling".
- ◇ Washing machine: Sides form a circle of arms, centre turns the head wildly like the laundry.
- ◇ Seal: Centre makes seal with noise, sides make the waves with hands.
- ◇ Statue: Centre poses as a statue, and sides kneel down and take photos.
- ◇ Duck: Centre makes a duck's beak and quacks, all three wag their bottoms.
- ◇ Fireman: Centre makes a hose with his arms, sides pump water.
- ◇ Hen: Centre bends down and pretends to lay an egg, sides catch the eggs and lay them in a basket.
- ◇ Cat: Centre says "meow, meow" and bounces lightly backwards and forwards, sides rub theirs heads on the 'cat' and purr.
- ◇ Milk the cow: Centre places both feet and hands on the floor with his bottom in the air, sides (the milk maids) pretend to milk the cow.
- ◇ Grilled chicken: Centre turns around in a circle, sides turn the spit.
- ◇ Cassette player: Centre sings a song, sides spin around on the spot, representing the rollers in the cassette.
- ◇ Cook: Centre is the cook and stirs around in the pot, sides make a large pot with their arms.
- ◇ Sandwich: Centre stands up straight, sides hug the middle player.

# 5. Climbing and Swinging: Jungle Gym Games

The very minute a child spots a jungle gym the response is a dash in that direction to climb, swing, slide, hang and experience the full joy of play. The great thing about jungle gyms is that the appeal does not lessen across a large age span – children from the age of 1 to 10 all seem to equally love the thrill of playing on a climbing frame. In addition to children's great love for this simple piece of playground equipment are the many health benefits associated with jungle gym play, such as the building up of muscle tone, coordination, balance and confidence.

Children who regularly play on jungle gyms are developing and learning to utilise their large muscle groups. They are learning the capacity of their muscles, how to manoeuvre their bodies in the most proactive ways, to coordinate their movements smoothly and to balance effectively. It is also a proven fact that children who are physically strong are more comfortable with their bodies. Kids that play on jungle gyms are, therefore, generally more confident and rarely miss out on activities due to fear, which, if not addressed, can become an issue in adulthood.

Therapists recognize jungle gym play as the best form of developmental play structure for young children. This form of free play encourages children to imagine scenarios in which they are a part of on their jungle gym like a pirate ship on the stormy seas, a princess' castle or a witches' kitchen. They are encouraged to use their imagination and creativity to produce their own form of fun play. Developmental play, learning to share and the use of the imagination are essentials to growing up. So, let's climb and swing and play some games.

# Angel on Earth

About the game:       An all-time favourite German playground game.
In the classroom:     A fun game for players of different ages.

Number of players:    5-20
Equipment:            none
Duration:             unlimited
Preparation:          none

*How to play:*

All players except the catcher spread out on the climbing frame.

The catcher now runs under and next to the climbing frame and tries to catch one of the players, while all players move on the climbing frame. The catcher can try to reach onto the scaffolding, but he is not allowed to step on the scaffolding.

The catcher must catch with his eyes closed. If possible, the other players should not be on the ground because the catcher has the opportunity to call "Angel on Earth". The other players answer "nobody" or say the name of the players who are on the ground. If a player is on the ground at the call, the two players switch roles and the player becomes the new catcher. If the catcher finds a player, he has to touch him and the roles are also swapped.

Make sure that the catcher does not call out every few seconds, because then the other players won't move anymore. Also, the other players should warn the catcher before he bumps into anything. Because the other children have to move, they tell the catcher through the noises they make where they are or that someone is currently on the ground.

The catcher can also call out "ice time" or "summer time". During ice time, he is allowed to open his eyes for five seconds and the other players must freeze and not move during this time. During summer time, the catcher is allowed to catch with his eyes open for ten seconds. There are other commands that the players can agree on, such as:

- "light house" – the catcher opens his eyes and revolves around himself once
- "tomato" – each player says his/her name
- "lemon" – each player makes a funny noise

# Fire, Water, Storm

| About the game: | This is an all-time-favourite game of German children. |
| In the Classroom: | Players practice English words for weather conditions. |

| Number of players: | 5-20 or as many as fit on the climbing frame |
| Equipment: | none |
| Duration: | unlimited |
| Preparation: | none |

*How to play:*

One person is the caller. Depending on the word they call out, players must perform specific actions. All players run around; no one is allowed to stand still. The players must perform an appropriate movement for each weather warning. Whoever performs a movement last, must leave the game. The game continues until one person is left and deemed the winner. Here are some appropriate movements for the various weather alerts:

- ✧ Fire: Players lay down flat on the ground, arms protecting their head, OR they hold on to something made of metal.
- ✧ Water: Players climb up on an object such as a climbing frame, bench or tree to escape the rushing water; no one is allowed to touch the ground.
- ✧ Storm: Players hold on tight to something to avoid being swept away by strong winds OR they lie flat on their stomach on the ground.
- ✧ Lightning: Curl up into a small ball on the floor to avoid a lightning strike.
- ✧ Rain: Players make an umbrella with theirs hands over their heads.
- ✧ Sun: Players lay on their backs OR form sunglasses with their hands.
- ✧ Ice: Players stop dead in their movements.

The leader can add further 'emergency situations', such as earth quakes and hurricanes or other fun words and think of required movements. The game can also be played around spring time to practice specific vocabulary. Here are some ideas:

- ✧ Bubble gum: Two players connect with one another.
- ✧ Rock: Players crouch on the ground.
- ✧ Easter bunny: Players make ears with their hands.
- ✧ Daffodil/Tulip: Players form a flower with their hands.
- ✧ Bee: Players flutter with their hands like wings.

# The Floor is Lava

| | |
|---|---|
| About the game: | The English version of the game Angel on Earth. |
| In the classroom: | A fun break time activity. |
| | |
| Number of players: | 10-20 |
| Equipment: | a climbing frame on a playground or furniture in a room |
| Duration: | 10 minutes |
| Preparation: | none |

*How to play:*

In this game the players pretend that the floor or ground is made of lava (or any other lethal substance, such as acid or quicksand), and thus must avoid touching the ground, as touching the ground would 'kill' the player who did so. Players must stay off the ground and on the play equipment. When played inside, the players stand on furniture.

Typically, any player starts the game just by shouting "The floor is lava!" Any player remaining on the floor in the next few seconds would be 'out'.

The players generally may not remain still and are required to move around on the climbing frame or from one piece of furniture to the next. This is due to some people saying that the furniture is acidic, sinking or in some other way time-limited in its use. The players must avoid stepping on the floor by staying on raised platforms, while 'it' (sometimes referred to as the 'lava monster') can walk across the floor and attempt to tag other players.

In some versions, the 'monster' is not allowed to touch certain obstacles, such as wooden platforms or may only touch objects of a certain colour. The 'monster' must navigate across structures such as playground slides, monkey bars, ropes courses, etc. instead of the main platform.

*Variations:*

There often are tasks, items or places that can 'regenerate' lost body parts or health. These could be embarrassing tasks, or simple things like finding a particular person. Players can also set up obstacles such as padded chairs to make the game more challenging and make it an obstacle course.

# 6. The Joy of Jumping: Skipping and Hopscotch

Skipping is one of the most popular games at the playgrounds in the UK. Many schools have skipping workshops that teach the children some tricks like Double Dutch, Pretzel, Stalk, Can-Can, Windscreen Wiper and Double Skipping.

There is so much joy in jumping. Moreover, skipping and playing hopscotch offer a range of benefits for both children and adults such as physical exercise. Hopping, jumping and balancing in hopscotch and skipping provides a great workout for the legs, improving strength, coordination, balance and cardiovascular fitness. The precise footwork required in both games enhances motor skills and spatial awareness. Hopping on one foot and navigating the grid or the skipping rope helps improve balance and coordination.

Moreover, the games are great for social interaction. Skipping and hopscotch are usually played with friends or in groups, fostering social interaction, teamwork and friendly competition. Not to forget, the games are great for mental stimulation. Planning the next hop and strategizing to avoid stepping on the lines and ropes engages the brain and enhances cognitive skills. There are many classic skipping rhymes that players sing, such as this one:

Teddy Bear, Teddy Bear, turn around; Teddy Bear, Teddy Bear, touch the ground.
Teddy Bear, Teddy Bear, show your shoe; Teddy Bear, Teddy Bear, that will do!
Teddy Bear, Teddy Bear, go upstairs; Teddy Bear, Teddy Bear, say your prayers.
Teddy Bear, Teddy Bear, turn out the lights; Teddy Bear, Teddy Bear, say goodnight!

# Double Dutch

About the game:            A jumping game with two long ropes.
In the classroom:           It trains coordination, stamina and the ability to react.

Number of players:          at least 3
Equipment:                2 long jump ropes, ca. 3.5m long
Duration:                  unlimited
Preparation:              none

*How to play:*

Double Dutch is a game in which two long jump ropes turning in opposite directions are jumped by one or more players jumping simultaneously.

It involves at least three people: one or more jumping, and two turning the ropes. Two of them have two ropes in their hands, which are loosely stretched between them. Both have one end of each rope in each hand. Both begin at the same time to swing the rope towards the middle in an arm movement with one hand and then start swinging the second rope towards the middle with a slight delay. The left arm moves clockwise, the right arm moves in the opposite direction. The players have to keep their arms still so that the swing comes from the fixed wrists and the speed can be increased without particularly exerting themselves.

The rope jumper now jumps between the ropes and must jump over the two ropes in various figures without touching them. The jumper performs tricks that may involve gymnastics or breakdance and incorporate fancy foot movements.

The simplest version of Double Dutch jumping is not hopping, but walking. Stand side-ways to the rope, which means that the respective rope comes from one side and the other at very short distances. The best way to do this is to pull your knees forward as you jump, as if you were jogging in place. Adapt your speed to the rotation of the rope. You can take a breath in the millisecond in which the ropes to your right and left are halfway up from you. Overall, you will be surrounded by the movements of both ropes. It looks like you are jumping in an ellipse and you are jumping around in it. You can only achieve special tricks such as a spin or an extravagant jump in the air when the ropes are halfway up the side.

*Did you know?*

The game probably originated among Dutch immigrants in New York City. The modern sport originated in the 1970s with NYPD officers Ulysses Williams and David Walker, who founded the National Double Dutch League (NDDL) and formalized the rules. The first official competition was held in 1974. Double Dutch competitions are categorized as compulsory, freestyle and speed rope.

# French Skipping

|                      |                                                          |
|----------------------|----------------------------------------------------------|
| About the game:      | A kids favourite, also called Chinese Jump Rope.         |
| In the classroom:    | A great activity for a short break.                      |
|                      |                                                          |
| Number of players:   | 3 players, 2 people to hold the rope and one to jump     |
| Equipment:           | a piece of elastic (2 cm wide and 3 metres in length)    |
| Duration:            | as long as you like to jump                              |
| Preparation:         | none                                                     |

*How to play:*

Tie the ends of the elastic together to make a loop. The two rope holders stand with the elastic around their ankles, their legs 30 cm apart, ca. 1.5 m away from each other. The 'jumper' starts by standing inside the loop performing a series of jumps, counting or chanting rhymes. If the jumper gets through the whole series of jumps without missing or landing in the wrong place, they move up to the next level. If the jumper makes a mistake, another player gets a turn. When finished, the height of the elastic is raised to knees, then thighs, then waist.

Basic French Skipping consists of the following series of jumps or hops: IN, OUT, SIDE, SIDE, ON, IN, OUT. (IN: both feet inside the ropes; OUT: both feet outside the ropes, one foot on either side; SIDE: both feet on one side of the ropes. In the side-side steps, the player hops first to one side, then over both ropes to the other side; ON: the player jumps and places one foot on top of each rope.)

*Skipping rhymes:*

Chocolate cake, when you bake,
how many minutes will you take?
One, two, three, four.

Charlie Chaplin sat on a pin
How many inches did it go in?
One, two, three, four.

Old Mrs Mason broke her basin
On the way to London Station.
How much did it cost?
One, two, three, four.'

England, Ireland, Scotland, Wales
Inside, outside, inside, on!'

How to jump on the numbers:

ONE: jump up, land with left foot outside the elastic loop and your right foot inside;
TWO: jump up and land with both feet together inside the elastic loop;
THREE: jump up and land with both feet outside the elastic loop;
FOUR: jump up and land sideways to the elastic, with your left foot on top of the back elastic and your right foot in front of the front elastic.

# Hopscotch

| | |
|---|---|
| About the game: | A traditional game played all over the world. |
| In the classroom: | Children can learn numbers while hopping. |

| | |
|---|---|
| Number of players: | any number |
| Equipment: | none |
| Duration: | unlimited |
| Preparation: | none |

*How to play:*

This traditional game involves hopping or jumping on one foot through a series of numbered squares or boxes, usually drawn with chalk on the ground.

Before you start, use a piece of chalk to draw a hopscotch grid on a flat surface. The grid consists of a series of numbered squares or boxes, usually arranged in a linear or snail-like pattern. The you decide on a throwing marker. Each player needs a small object, such as a pebble or a bean-bag, to use as a throwing marker.

Then start hopping. The first player stands at the starting line and throws their marker into the first square. The player hops through the grid, skipping the square with the marker. They must hop on one foot when landing in a single square and use both feet when landing in a square with two adjacent boxes. Once the player reaches the end of the grid, they turn around and hop back, retrieving their marker on the way.

The next player repeats the same steps, starting from where the previous player left off. Players take turns until everyone has completed the course.

*Did you know?*

It is attested that an ancient form of hopscotch was played by Roman children and soldiers. However, the first recorded references to the game in the English-speaking world date to the late 17th century, when is gained popularity in England. It was known as 'Scotch-hoppers' or 'Scotch-hopping', and the squares were often marked with numbers or letters. The game was not only played by children but also enjoyed by adults as a form of entertainment.

# 8. Let's Get Loud: Singing Games

Singing games have been played for many generations and are great fun. A singing game is an activity based on a specific verse or rhyme, typically associated with a set of actions and movements. Singing games have been studied by folklorists, ethnologists and psychologists and are seen as important part of childhood culture. Some of them originated in pagan survival rituals and have been evolved by children and adults over many generations.

A variety of roles have been attributed to singing games, including exploring language, allowing acceptable criticism and to regularise and ritualise play and other behaviour. Most singing games tend to be co-operative rather than competitive and communal rather than hierarchical. They can be a great way to break the ice and get to know each other – whether in the classroom or at camp.

There are many reasons why singing games belong in the classroom. With singing games, it becomes easy to teach different musical concepts. They are fun and inspire a feeling of community, because these games provide children with the opportunity to sing as a group and on their own. They are easy to set up and require no or few props and no accompaniment. They are a welcome counterpoint to exercises that require sitting and concentration. Often, they provide an opportunity for children to connect with their heritage and that of others.

Many songs inspire kids to run, jump and wiggle as they sing. The following pages offer a small selection of English singing games that come with silly movements.

# Head, Shoulders, Knees and Toes

| | |
|---|---|
| About the game: | A traditional English children's song. |
| In the classroom: | A great song introducing learners to parts of the body. |

| | |
|---|---|
| Number of players: | any number |
| Equipment: | none |
| Duration: | 5 minutes |
| Preparation: | none |

*How to play:*

There is only one verse with lyrics similar to those below. The second line repeats the first line both in words and in melody, the third line has a rising tone, and the fourth line repeats the first two. Children might dance while they sing the song and touch their head, shoulders, knees and toes in sequence to the words.

*Lyrics:*

Head, shoulders, knees and toes, knees and toes,
Head, shoulders, knees and toes, knees and toes,
And eyes and ears and mouth and nose.
Head, shoulders, knees and toes, knees and toes.

To make it more fun, the lyrics can also be sung in reverse, like this:
Toes, knees and shoulders, head, shoulders, head.
Toes, knees and shoulders, head, shoulders, head
And nose and mouth and ears and eyes,
Toes, knees and shoulders, head, shoulders, head.

Each verse is repeated, with one word being omitted each time, just touching their body parts, without saying the word. For example:

Verse 2: ----, shoulders, knees, and toes
Verse 3: ----, ----, knees, and toes
Verse 4: ----, ----, ----, and toes
Verse 5: ----, ----, ----, and ----

This pattern continues until all the words are omitted. The last verse consists of no actual singing or singing all lyrics, but sometimes at a much faster tempo.

# Hello, My Name is Joe (and I Work in a Button Factory)

About the game:          The song is a favourite for parties and playgrounds.
In the classroom:         Great for practicing new words for body parts.

Number of players:       any number
Equipment:             none
Duration:               10-15 minutes
Preparation:           none

*How to play:*

The song begins innocently enough. The singer introduces himself by saying, "Hello, my name is Joe / and I work in a button factory." You can get silly with the children and have them push the button with their head, nose, ears, buttocks or other body parts. Each time a body part is mentioned, pantomime pushing a button with that body part (or 'wave' the body part if you say "turn"). Each body part is added to the body part before until both hands, both feet, head and tongue are all moving!

*The Lyrics:*

Hello, my name is Joe,
and I work in a button factory,
I've got a wife, a dog and a family. (OR I've got a wife and one kid)
One day my boss said to me, "Are you busy, Joe?"
And I said, "No!"
"Then push this button with your right hand."

... "Then push this button with your left hand."

... "Then push this button with your left foot."

... "Then push this button with your head."

... "Then push this button with your tongue."

Hello, my name is Joe,
and I work in a button factory,
I've got a wife, a dog and a family.
One day my boss said to me, "Are you busy, Joe?"
And I said, "Yes!"

# Here We Go with the Big Fat Pony

| | |
|---|---|
| About the game: | This is an active game for groups of any size and age. |
| In the classroom: | Singing a silly song always brings fun into the group. |

| | |
|---|---|
| Number of players: | any number |
| Equipment: | none |
| Duration: | 5 minutes |
| Preparation: | none |

*How to play:*

The players are standing in a circle, not too crowded so that everybody can move freely. All together sing the song, clapping their hands. The facilitator starts to run around inside the circle and sings the song: "Here we go with the big fat pony. Here we go with the big fat pony. Here we go with the big fat pony, early in the morning" (using the melody of the song "What shall we do with a drunken sailor").

With the last word of the verse, the person running inside the circle stops in front of a person standing in the circle and starts dancing and singing with her: "Front, front, front, my baby. Back, back, back, my baby. Side, side, side, my baby, early in the morning," doing the activities and dance moves. Then the person dancing takes the person in front of her and both start running around in the circle singing.

Again, with the last word of the verse, they each stop in front of another person. They both dance again, and when finished, they take the person with them to run around in the circle. This continues as long as all participants are running around and singing the verse.

*Lyrics:*

Here we go with the big fat pony,
here we go with the big fat pony,
here we go with the big fat pony,
early in the morning.
Front, front, front, my baby,
back, back, back, my baby,
side, side, side, my baby,
early in the morning.

*Movements:*

➢ active players are running around the circle
➢ they select a previously passive player
➢ rhythmically clapping on your thighs
➢ rhythmically clapping on your buttocks
➢ shaking your hips to the left and right

*Variations:*

You can modify the dance moves and the verse but keep it simple. In bigger groups, you can start with more than one person to quicken the pace.

# If You're Happy and You Know it

| | |
|---|---|
| About the game: | A popular traditional repetitive children's song. |
| In the classroom: | A fun song to bring movement into the classroom. |

| | |
|---|---|
| Number of players: | any number |
| Equipment: | none |
| Duration: | 5 minutes |
| Preparation: | none |

*How to play:*

There are many versions of the lyrics; a popular version goes like this:

"If you're happy and you know it, clap your hands.
If you're happy and you know it, clap your hands.
If you're happy and you know it, and you really want to show it;
If you're happy and you know it, clap your hands."

This verse is usually followed by more verses which follow the same pattern but express other emotions such as:

"If you're angry and you know it, stomp your feet!"

"If you're sad and you know it, cry out loud!"

"If you're scared and you know it, run and hide!"

"If you're embarrassed and you know it, hide your face."

"If you're sleepy and you know it, stretch and yawn."

"If you're in love and you know it, blow a kiss."

There are many variations on the substance of the first verse, including:

"... shout/say, 'Hooray'!"
"... slap your knees!"
"... clap your hands!"
"... turn around!"
"... snap your fingers!"
"... nod your head!""... tap your toe!"
"... honk your nose!"
"... pat your head!"
"... pull your ears!"
"... give a whistle!"

# Once an Austrian Went Yodelling

| | |
|---|---|
| About the game: | A fun song for singers of all ages. |
| In the classroom: | Children love the noises and movements of the song. |

| | |
|---|---|
| Number of players: | any number |
| Equipment: | none |
| Duration: | 10 minutes |
| Preparation: | none |

*How to play:*

Sing the song and make the noises and movements. Think of new movements.

1. Once an Austrian went yodelling on a mountain so high,
   When along came an avalanche interrupting his cry.
   Yodelay dee:
   Yodel-lay-hee-hee, yodel-lay-hee-hoo (rumble, rumble),
           (say "rumble, rumble", shake as if in an earthquake)
   Yodel-lay-hee-hee, yodel-lay-hee-hoo (rumble, rumble),
   Yodel-lay-hee-hee, yodel-lay-hee-hoo (rumble, rumble),
   Yodelay hee-hay-dee-hoo.

2. Once an Austrian went yodelling on a mountain so high,
   when along came a skier interrupting his cry.
   Yodelay dee:
   Yodel-lay-hee-hee, yodel-lay-hee-hoo (rumble, rumble; swish, swish),
           (say "swish, swish", flat palms swoop downwards),
   Yodel-lay-hee-hee, yodel-lay-hee-hoo (rumble, rumble; swish, swish),
   Yodel-lay-hee-hee, yodel-lay-hee-hoo (rumble, rumble; swish; swish),
   Yodelay hee-hay-dee-hoo.

3. ... when along came a grizzly bear interrupting his cry – roar or grr

4. ... when along came a dinosaur interrupting his cry – !!!

5. ... when along came a Guernsey cow interrupting his cry – moo, moo

6. ... when along came a St. Bernard interrupting his cry – arf, arf

7. ... when along came a milking maid interrupting his cry – tss, tss

8. ... when along came a pretty girl interrupting his cry – smack, smack (make kissing noise, throw kiss with left and right hand.)

# Round De Doo Bop (Going to Kentucky)

| | |
|---|---|
| About the game: | This is an easy one with a really fun song to go with it. |
| In the classroom: | In this game kids love to wiggle with total abandon. |

| | |
|---|---|
| Number of players: | any number |
| Equipment: | none |
| Duration: | 10 minutes |
| Preparation: | none |

*How to play:*

Players stand in a circle with one player in the middle. Each line of the song has an accompanying movement. Toward the end, the player in the middle turns in a circle while pointing. When the song ends, whoever the player in the centre is pointing at becomes 'it' to stand in the middle for the next round. Here are the lyrics and movements: Players in the circle join hands and walk around the circle; player in the middle dances.

*Lyrics:*
We're going to Kentucky,
we're going to the fair
to see the Señorita
with flowers in her hair.
So, shake it, shake it, shake it,
shake it if you dare./all you can
Shake it like a milkshake,
and shake it here to there/do the
best you can.
Oh, roll it to the bottom
and roll it to the top,
and turn around and turn around
and turn around and stop!

*Movements:*

➢ players stand in place and do a shaking dance

➢ players roll arms and bend down
➢ players roll arms and stretch up
➢ player in the middle covers his eyes with one hand, puts out the other arm with finger pointing, and turns around in place until the word "stop!"

# Singing in the Rain

| | |
|---|---|
| About the game: | This is a singing and dancing game for groups. |
| In the classroom: | It contains lots of silly movements and actions. |

| | |
|---|---|
| Number of players: | any size |
| Equipment: | none |
| Duration: | 15-30 minutes |
| Preparation: | none |

*How to play:*

First, the following verse of the song is sung, using some lyrics of the song *Singin' in the Rain* by Gene Kelly: I'm singing in the rain,
just singing in the rain,
what a glorious feeling
I'm happy again.

Then the leader interrupts using these words: "Hold it, hold it!"

The text is repeated by all participants. Then, the leader commands and demonstrates a special movement: "Hands up", demonstrating the command by stretching his hands forwards.

The group repeats his command and does as demonstrated. Then, everybody is dancing where he is standing (swing one's hips) and singing the following text:

A zumzaza, A zumzaza, A zumzazaza-aha
A zumzaza, A zumzaza, A zumzazaza-aha

After that, the next round is started. Again, the lyrics are sung. Then, the leader repeats all movements and adds another one (so, one movement in the first round, two in the second, three in the third, etc.).

The following movements are suggested; remember that they must be kept while dancing, what is especially funny for "tongue out". Of course, you can add other movements.

- ➢ Hands up – stretch hands forwards
- ➢ Thumbs up – stretch your arms forwards, thumbs up
- ➢ Elbows back – press elbows against hips, but stretch forearm still forwards
- ➢ Knees together – press your knees together
- ➢ Head back – throw your head back
- ➢ Tongue out – stick your tongue out

# 8. Guessing Games, Riddles and Other Activities

Riddles, brain teasers, puzzles and scavenger hunts with all kinds of challenges are all-time-favourites of children, youth and adults alike. Enjoying oneself while exercising the brain has been a favourite activity of many of us. If you are looking for a way to pass the time, get a little smarter or have some fun, these are the right games for you.

There all kinds of riddles, lateral puzzles, guessing games, card tricks and other party games that are fun to play and well suited to impress friends, classmates, students or family members. In the classroom, these games provide fun for all learners, as they allow them to discover patterns on their own. They are also educational, as player will develop observational skills.

This chapter offers a small selection of riddles, acting games, memory games, guessing games and other fun activities such as relay races, cooperative games and scavenger hunts. Depending on their level of difficulty these games are well suited for classroom, camp and campus. You can always adjust the theme, level of difficulty or pace according to the age of the players and the setting.

Have fun guessing and gaming.

# Airplane Game

| | |
|---|---|
| About the game: | A cooperative game for all ages. |
| In the classroom: | It can be played with any size of group. |

| | |
|---|---|
| Number of players: | 2-20 |
| Equipment: | a blindfold |
| Duration: | 10 minutes |
| Preparation: | none |

*How to play:*

Select one player from your group to be the airplane, one to be the navigator, and the rest of the players are the trees. In a small designated area (the runway) have the trees spread out and take root (they cannot move). The airplane is blindfolded and the navigator gives clear step by step directions to get the airplane across the runway without crashing into a tree. The navigator can give only one direction at a time.

*Variations:*

There are many variations of this game, such as a blind walk through an obstacle course. Set some plastic cups on the floor and have them spaced apart randomly. One person is blindfolded. That person has to walk through the cups from one end to the other without touching any cup, while the rest have to guide him through by verbal communication only. Take turns under the blindfold and see how the communication skills start developing.

You can also play the game in teams and see what groups gives the clearer instructions for guiding the blindfolded player through the field.

# Charades

<table>
<tr><td>About the game:</td><td>A word guessing game for groups of all ages.</td></tr>
<tr><td>In the classroom:</td><td>A great game to practice all kinds of vocabulary.</td></tr>
</table>

<table>
<tr><td>Number of players:</td><td>2-20</td></tr>
<tr><td>Equipment:</td><td>word cards</td></tr>
<tr><td>Duration:</td><td>10 minutes</td></tr>
<tr><td>Preparation:</td><td>write terms on cards</td></tr>
</table>

*How to play:*

Begin with preparing a bowl of words, phrases, songs, titles of books or films, or other terms. In turn, each player draws a slip from the bowl and acts out the phrase shown using hand signals and body motions but no spoken words.

Players then try to guess the word/title/phrase. The player giving the correct answer is allocated a point. You may use a timer to keep rounds short and succinct.

When playing with a larger crowd, divide into teams before playing. If a team does not guess the acted phrase correctly within the time limit, the other team can try to guess the phrase and steal the point. The player or team with the most points wins the game.

*Variations:*

There are several standard categories and accompanying actions used in Charades, such as the following:

Movie title: Pretend to be turning the reel of an old-fashioned movie camera.
TV show title: Draw a rectangle in the air with fingers to indicate a TV.
Song title: Draw your hand away from your mouth while pretending to sing.
Book title: Pretend to open a book by opening your hands.
Play title: Indicate a stage curtain opening by drawing hands apart.
Quotes & phrases: Make air quotes with fingers.

*Did you know?*

Originating in France in the 18th century, the game of Charades evolved from a riddle-based game where participants described the individual syllables of a word and its full definition for others to solve.

# Kim's Game or Memory Game

| | |
|---|---|
| About the game: | A game often played by scouts and other groups. |
| In the classroom: | It develops a person's memory and observation skills. |
| | |
| Number of players: | 2-20 |
| Equipment: | 10-20 small objects (e.g., band-aid, toothpick, pencil, toys), a dish towel or piece of cloth to cover items |
| Duration: | 10 minutes |
| Preparation: | place objects in a marked area |

*How to play:*

Place the collection of items on a table, a tray or a marked field on the ground (ca. 1m x 1 m). Have each person look over and memorize the collection. Cover all the items with a cloth and have each person write down as many items as they can remember. After an allotted time (10 seconds to 1 minute, depending on the number of items), remove the cloth. The person who listed the most items wins.

You can increase or decrease the number of items used. After the items are covered, you can ask question, such as: What is the smallest/largest object? Go and find one item you saw in another part of the playground, room or building.

*Variations:*

When played with young players, you can simplify the game. Rather than being asked to list all the objects, the players are asked to identify one missing object that is removed from the tray. You can also add an item that wasn't there before and ask which item is new to the collection. When played in a room or playing area, the guesser can move away from that area until one item is removed. When returning, all the other players ask "What's missing?"

The game can be used as a basis for a scavenger or for practicing any topic in class. During Christmas, you can use objects such as candles, baubles, cookies, a Gingerbread man and a ribbon. In winter, you can use a stick, a pinecone, a stone, a mitten and other objects kids find on the playground.

*Did you know?*

The name 'Kim' is derived from Rudyard Kipling's 1901 novel *Kim*, in which the protagonist plays the game during his training as a spy.

# Little Green Wizard

| | |
|---|---|
| About the game: | In this guessing game everybody is involved. |
| In the classroom: | Players practice talking about people. |

| | |
|---|---|
| Number of players: | 10-20 |
| Equipment: | none |
| Duration: | 10 minutes |
| Preparation: | none |

*How to play:*

The players are sitting in a circle. One player (knowing the solution) starts the game by saying: "I am a small green wizard because I ...", and he offers some explanation why he is a small green wizard.

Then, the next player does the same thing. All players knowing the solution clarify whether his statement was correct or not. The target of all players is to find out the system what makes a statement valid or not.

Any player guessing to know the solution do not disclose it, but just participate in the game and try to play along correctly.

And what is the solution?

The statement must be correct not for you, but for your right neighbour. If the line was "I'm a little green wizard because I have black hair", the right neighbour must have black hair (and not the player talking).

In the classroom learners can practice new vocabulary such as words for body parts, hobbies, colours, favourite animals or food.

*Variations:*

Another popular riddle is *Green Glass Door*. Some things can go through the green glass door, but other things can't, for example:

> A puppy can go through the green glass door, but a dog can't.
> A kitten can go through, but a cat can't.
> A spoon can go through, but a fork can't.
> A pool can go through, but a lake can't.

What else can go through the green glass door?

# Red Letter

| | |
|---|---|
| About the game: | Players move forward on particular letters. |
| In the classroom: | Young players can practice the alphabet. |

| | |
|---|---|
| Number of players: | 3 or more people |
| Equipment: | none |
| Duration: | 10 minutes |
| Preparation: | none |

*How to play:*

Choose one person in your group to be the 'letter-picker'. This person is posted at the far end of the designated play area. The others gather in a horizontal line at the opposite end. The letter-picker picks one letter of the alphabet to be the 'red letter', telling the other participants what it is. The point of the 'red letter' will become clear as the game gets underway.

After making sure that the other participants are ready, the 'letter-picker' calls out a letter of the alphabet. This can be any letter, including the 'red letter'. If the letter is not the 'red letter', the participants (not the letter-picker) take x number of steps forward, depending on the number of that letter in their full name. If the letter called out was 'e', and the person had 4 'e's in their name, the person would take 4 steps forward. On the other hand, if the 'red letter' chosen was 'e', and a person starts to move forward, they have to return to the beginning. Therefore, the objective is to get to the same end as the letter-picker first, and to remember not to move when the 'red letter' is called.

The first person to get to the same end as the letter-picker gets the prize that is available and the honour of being the letter-picker in the next game.

*Variations:*

Other twists on the game may include: doing a forfeit if you move forward when the 'red letter' is called; instead of stepping forward, hop, skip or jump; barring middle-names from the game; having the 'red letter' as a letter that is in nobody's name, or is not likely to be called out; sudden death – the letter-picker can only call a letter once, but the 'red letter' may be called at any time.

# Relay Race

| | |
|---|---|
| About the game: | In this game equal teams race to achieve a task. |
| In the classroom: | It provides team competition for different occasions. |

| | |
|---|---|
| Number of players: | at least 10 |
| Equipment: | depending on the race |
| Duration: | 10-20 minutes |
| Preparation: | none |

*How to play:*

Relay races are racing competitions where members of a team take turns completing parts of race course or performing a certain action. There are many different relay races for various ages and situations. Warm summer days are perfect for outdoor relay races; others can be played inside. Here are a few suggestions; for each race, split the group into teams and have them stand in a single-file line.

*Balloon Race:* The leader of each line must pass a balloon through their legs to the player behind them. That player passes the balloon overhead to the next player. Repeat this pattern until the balloon gets all the way to the end of the line. The last player runs back to the front of the line and pops the balloon to win.

*Newspaper Relay Race:* Each player has two pieces of newspaper (or towels). During the race, the runner puts one piece of paper down and steps on it. Then they put the next piece of newspaper down (while picking up the other) and steps on it. The players continue in this fashion until they get to the next player. Once they cross the line, that player takes their newspapers and does the same thing going back until they cross the finish line for the next teammate.

*Fill-it Water Race:* Set up an obstacle course using whatever is available – tables, chairs, large rocks, etc. Give each team a plastic cup and a full bucket of water. Team members take turns filling the cup and racing to an empty bucket at the end of the course. The first team to fill the empty bucket wins the game.

*Sponge Race:* Place a bucket with water and a sponge in the front of each line and an empty bucket at the back. Each team must transport the water using the sponge from the front of the line to the back. The last person in line squeezes the filled sponge into the bucket and runs to the front, where the task begins again. The team that manages to pass the most water before the time is up wins.

*Pass the Water:* Similar to the sponge race, a plastic cup filled with water passes from one person to another from a full bucket at the beginning of the line to an empty one at the end. The person passing the water must use their teeth and have their hands clasped behind their back.

# Scavenger Hunt

|  |  |
|---|---|
| About the game: | Scavenger hunts are great fun for children of all ages. |
| In the classroom: | Kids boost observation skills and practice new words. |
| | |
| Number of players: | 3 or more people |
| Equipment: | paper and pencil, pictures or different objects |
| Duration: | 15 minutes or more |
| Preparation: | write hunt clues |

*How to play:*

Create a list of specific items for participants to find. Set a start and end time and decide whether participants should work individually or in teams. Consider prizes, rewards or incentives for top finishers. The goal is to be the first to complete the list or to complete the most items on that list. You can match a clever phrasing that indicates where the item is located but in a somewhat mystifying way that requires some problem-solving. Writing scavenger hunt clues can be great fun.

There are many different ways to organize scavenger hunts. A treasure hunt is another name for the game, but it may involve following a series of clues to find objects or a single prize in a particular order.

*Variations:*

There are countless themes for scavenger hunts, and it's so much fun to create your own specific hunt. Here are a few ideas:

*Letter Scavenger Hunt:* Have participants find items with a particular letter, for example the letter 'F': two feet, a flower, a frog, a fork, a fish, a fire truck.

*Book Scavenger Hunt:* Have participants find particular titles in a library.

*Nature or Playground Scavenger Hunt:* Have the participants find various items, such as three flowers that have a strong scent, a stick longer than your arm, an item smaller than your thumb, or something light enough to float on water.

*Did you know?*

According to game scholar Markus Montola, scavenger hunts evolved from ancient folk games. Large scavenger hunts are regularly held at American colleges and universities. An event organized in Ottawa, Canada, currently holds the Guinness World Record for the world's largest scavenger hunt with 2,732 participants.

# Wink Murder or Murder in the Dark

About the game:         A popular party game played all over the world.
In the classroom:       A great icebreaker game for new groups.

Number of players:      6-30; best played with about 10 players
Equipment:              none
Duration:               ca. 20 minutes
Preparation:            none

*How to play:*

One person is the picker and responsible for choosing both the murderer and the detective and will not play. All the players sit in a circle and close their eyes. The picker walks around the outside of the circle and chooses the murderer by tapping someone on the head one time. The detective is chosen by tapping someone on the head twice. Then everyone can open their eyes.

The detective moves to the middle of the circle. His goal is to determine who the murderer is as quickly as possible.

The murderer kills people by winking at them. When a player is killed, that player should lie down or leave the circle. (Many players like to make the killing dramatic by, for example, pretending they have been shot.)

The detective has three chances to guess who the murderer is. If the detective does not guess correctly, he remains the detective for the next round. If the detective does guess right, the murderer becomes the detective for the next round.

*Variations:*

In this version of the game, everyone other than the murderer is a detective. Once a detective thinks he has determined who the murderer is, he can alert the picker by rocking gently back and forth and then whispering the answer to the picker. If the player guesses incorrectly, he is killed. A player may challenge the murderer by approaching them and asking them directly.

In the variant known as *Murder Handshake,* the murderer kills by using a special handshake determined before the game begins. It is usually a scratching or tickling of the victim's palm as they give a handshake. This game starts with players walking around and routinely shaking hands as though greeting one another at a party. The murderer strikes by using the special handshake. It is recommended that victims do not 'die' immediately but take a few steps or shake hands with one or two other people before feigning death.

# Who Am I?

About the game:          A fun guessing game for many players.
In the classroom:       A great game for practicing new vocabulary

Number of players:     5-20
Equipment:           post-it notes or similar small paper
Duration:             10 minutes
Preparation:        Write an animal on post-its, a different one on each.

*How to play:*

Each player gets one of the post-its and sticks it to his forehead or his back. Of course, he should not read what term is written on it. All other players can read the term, but he cannot. Is everybody able to find out who he is?

All players sit in a circle or move around the playing area. They may ask each other yes/no questions that the other person must answer correctly in accordance to the 'personality' of the asking person. They may keep on asking one person as long as they get "yes" as an answer.

For example, 'Elephant' might ask: "I am grey?" The answer would be "Yes". He would continue: "I have got big ears and a trunk?" Advice: The correct question form 'Am I' can be used, but might be too difficult for young learners.

There are many possible questions that can be linked to specific topics in the EFL classroom, for example:

Jobs:    I'm a woman / man?
          I'm working in a building / in town / on a farm / at school?
          I cut hair / repair a car / drive a bus /
          I'm a hairdresser / mechanic / teacher / etc.

Animals: I'm big / small / green / brown / yellow / colourful?
          I live at a farm / in a zoo / in the jungle / in the house?
          I can jump / run very fast / climb up trees / dive?
          I eat grass / mice / meat / apples?

Fruit:    I am green / orange / yellow?
          I taste sweet / sour?
          I grow in a warm country / in the south / everywhere?

# 9. Through the Year: Seasonal Games

Whatever the weather and the season, playing games outside is always great fun. There are many games to play throughout the year – be it on the playground in spring, in the lakes or pools in summer or in the warm house in winter. Many of us remember exciting egg hunts during Easter time, flying a self-made kite in autumn or building unique snow sculptures in winter.

This chapter introduces a few games that can be played during special seasons throughout the years, such as Egg Hunt, Egg Rolling and Egg Tapping. Playing conkers in autumn is very British and, therefore, included in this chapter.

Many of the above-mentioned games can be adapted and played during the holiday season. Kim's Game can be played as Winter Kim, using objects found outside on the playground or in the woods in winter. Relay Races such as Balloon Race or Newspaper Race are great fun at a carnival or Halloween party.

During Christmas, there are games like Jingle Bell Toss or Candy Cane Hunt that are fun to play with family and friends. You can also play many games with a Christmas theme, such as Charade, Memory, Pictionary, Trivia and other guessing games. For the Stocking Guessing Game, for example, fill a stocking with small toys and Christmas items such as a candy cane, a bell, a toy car or a pinecone. Let the players feel the stocking and try to identify the contents. The player with the most correct guesses is the winner.

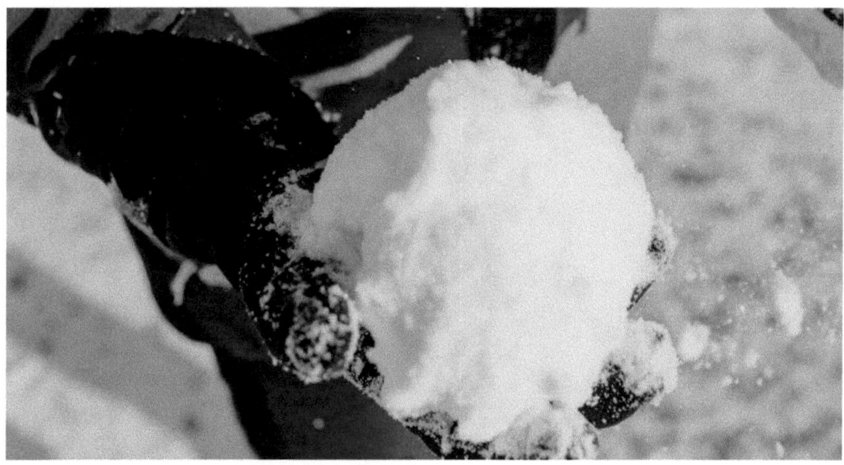

# Egg Hunt

| | |
|---|---|
| About the game: | A traditional game played with eggs at Easter. |
| In the classroom: | A fun activity for the last day of class. |
| | |
| Number of players: | at least 2 |
| Equipment: | hard-boiled coloured eggs or chocolate eggs |
| Duration: | unlimited |
| Preparation: | none |

*How to play:*

An egg hunt is a treasure hunt played at Easter during which children look for hidden decorated eggs or Easter eggs. Real hard-boiled eggs, which are typically dyed or painted, artificial eggs made of plastic filled with chocolate or candies, or foil-wrapped egg-shaped chocolates of various sizes are hidden in various places.

The game is often played outdoors, but can also be played indoors. The children typically collect the eggs in a basket. When the hunt is over, prizes may be given out for various achievements, such as the largest number of eggs collected, for the largest or smallest egg, for the most eggs of a specific colour.

Real eggs may further be used in egg tapping contests.

*Did you know?*

The egg was a symbol of the rebirth of the earth in pre-Christian celebrations of spring. In Christianity, Easter eggs symbolize the empty tomb of Jesus, from which he was resurrected.

The idea of the Easter Bunny to bring the Easter eggs has been known since the 17th century.

The world's largest Easter egg hunt took place in Winter Haven, Florida, where 501,000 eggs were hidden in a park and 9,753 children tried to find them all.

# Egg-and-Spoon Race

| | |
|---|---|
| About the game: | A traditional game played with eggs at Easter. |
| In the classroom: | A fun sporting event for players of any age. |

| | |
|---|---|
| Number of players: | at least 2 |
| Equipment: | hard-boiled coloured eggs or chocolate eggs |
| Duration: | 10-15 minutes |
| Preparation: | none |

*How to play:*

An egg-and-spoon race is a sporting event in which participants must balance an egg or similarly shaped item upon a spoon and race with it to the finishing line.

Competitors race either individually or in teams in the manner of a relay race. If the egg falls from the spoon then competitors may be required to stop, retrieve and reposition their egg, or to start again, or may even be disqualified. Due to the lesser penalty imposed for dropping the egg, and consequent encouragement of greater risk-taking, the first penalty scenario may result in a race that is faster overall. Common methods of cheating include sticking the egg to the spoon, or holding onto the egg with one finger.

For an extra challenge, contestants might carry the spoon with both hands, with their teeth, or have their hands tied behind their backs.

*Did you know?*

In 2013, the Australian Sally Pearson set the record for the fastest 100 metre egg-and-spoon race (16.59 seconds). A number of world records in egg-and-spoon racing are held by the New Yorker Ashrita Furman, including the fastest 100 metre egg-and-spoon race while holding the spoon in the mouth (25.13 seconds). In 1990 a runner completed the London Marathon in three hours forty-seven minutes while balancing a raw egg on a spoon.

# Egg Rolling

About the game:        A traditional game played with eggs at Easter.
In the classroom:       A fun activity for players of all ages.

Number of players:     at least 2
Equipment:            hard-boiled eggs
Duration:              10 minutes
Preparation:          none

*How to play:*

The Egg Roll is a race where players push an egg through the grass with a long-handled spoon. All players line up with their eggs and on the word "go", let the eggs roll down the hill.

There can be two types of Easter Egg Roll Game winners: One is the egg that has gone the furthers (curved lines don't count; it has to be furthest down the hill). This is relatively easy to determine, as it is a physical distance. No throwing! The second way to win is to determine which egg remains intact the most. As this might be rather subjective, make sure an independent judge has been nominated.

*Did you know?*

In the UK, the tradition of rolling decorated eggs down grassy hills goes back hundreds of years and is known as 'pace-egging'. Traditionally, the eggs were wrapped in onion skins and boiled to give them a mottled, gold appearance, and the children competed to see who could roll their egg the farthest.

There is an old Lancashire legend that says the broken eggshells should be crushed carefully afterward, or these would be stolen and used as boats by witches. The eggs were eaten on Easter Sunday or given out to pace-eggers – colourfully dressed characters who processed through the streets singing songs and collecting money as a tribute before performing traditional plays.

# Egg Tapping

| | |
|---|---|
| About the game: | Egg tapping, also known as egg fight, egg knocking, egg jarping, or egg wars, is a traditional Easter game. |
| In the classroom: | Kids might play this game during break time. |

| | |
|---|---|
| Number of players: | 2 |
| Equipment: | hard-boiled eggs |
| Duration: | 10 minutes |
| Preparation: | none |

*How to play:*

One player holds a hard-boiled egg and taps the egg of another participant with one's own egg in-tending to break the other's, without breaking one's own.

*Did you know?*

Egg tapping was already practiced in Mediaeval Europe.

In Sydney, Australia, there are competitions in egg tapping since 1974. Each Easter, the World Egg Jarping Championships have been held in Peterlee, England, since 1983. Often winners must eat their winning eggs to prove that the eggs are not of another material. This rule was introduced in 1984 following several competitors who were found to have painted wooden eggs. As with any other game, it has been a subject of cheating; eggs with cement, alabaster and even marble cores have been reported.

# Conkers

| | |
|---|---|
| About the game: | It is played using the seeds of horse chestnut trees. |
| In the classroom: | An interesting game for discussing cultural traditions. |

| | |
|---|---|
| Number of players: | 2 |
| Equipment: | conker threaded onto a piece of string (shoelace) |
| Duration: | 10 minutes |
| Preparation: | Drill a hole into a large conker using a nail or screwdriver, thread a piece of string (20-25 cm long) through it and secure the conker with knots at both ends. |

*How to Play:*

The game is played between two people, each with a conker hanging on a string wrapped around the hands of the opponents. They take turns hitting each other's conker using their own. One player lets the conker dangle on the full length of the string. The conker is held at the height your opponent chooses and is held perfectly still. The other player (the striker) wraps his conker string round his hand and takes his conker in the other hand and draws it back for the strike and swings their conker to hit it. A point is scored for a conker surviving a hit that causes the other one to break. The point is scored irrespective of whether the surviving conker was attacking or defending at the time. The game goes on in turns until one or other of the two conkers is completely destroyed.

If a player misses hitting his opponent's conker they are allowed up to two further goes. If the strings tangle, the first player to call 'strings' gets an extra shot/turn. If a player hits his opponent's conker in such a way that it completes a whole circle after being hit – known as 'round the world' – the player gets another go. If a player drops his conker or it is knocked out of his hand the other player can shout 'stamps' and jump on it; but should its owner first cry 'no stamps' then the conker, hopefully, remains intact.

The scoring of the game is considered to be a property of the conkers themselves. A new conker is a none-er, meaning that it has not defeated any others yet and thus has no score. As a conker accumulates points, its designation changes to reflect the total: a none-er becomes a one-er, then a two-er, and so on. A victorious conker assumes the score of all its victim's precedent foes.

*Did you know?*

On finding your first conker of the season, you should say: "Oddly oddly onker my first conker". This ensures good fortune throughout the coming season.

# Christmas Musical Chair Game

| | |
|---|---|
| About the game: | A traditional party game for all ages. |
| In the classroom: | It can be played inside and outside. |

| | |
|---|---|
| Number of players: | 10-15 |
| Equipment: | Christmas music, chairs |
| Duration: | 10 minutes |
| Preparation: | arrange a set of chairs in two rows |

*How to play:*

Musical chairs, also known as Trip to Jerusalem, is a game of elimination involving players, chairs and music. A set of chairs is arranged with one fewer chair than the number of players (for example, ten players would use nine chairs). While music plays, the contestants walk around the chairs. When the music stops abruptly, all players must find their own individual chair to sit on. The player who fails to sit on a chair is eliminated. One chair is then removed for the next round, and the process repeats until only one player remains and is declared the winner.

For the Christmas edition of the game, simply add Christmas music and play the traditional game. When played outside, instead of chairs you can use newspapers or hula hoops on/in which the contestants have to stand when the music stops.

*Variations:*

*Pass the Present:* While Christmas music is playing, a wrapped gift is passed around. When the music stops, whoever is left holding the package is out.

*Christmas Ornament Musical Chairs:* Cut ornament shapes from construction paper. The players walk while the music is playing. When the music stops, each must stand on an ornament cut-out. Whoever cannot find one to stand on is out.

# Snowball Relay Race

About the game: An action-packed running game for all ages.
In the classroom: It can be played inside and outside.

Number of players: 10-15
Equipment: a bag of cotton balls, 2 plastic spoons, 2 buckets
Duration: 10 minutes
Preparation: none

*How to play:*

Relay races are games where equal teams race to achieve a task. Relay race games provide team competition for many different occasions – day camps, school recesses and outdoor parties as well as many other group get-togethers.

The goal in this fun relay race is to move snowballs (cotton balls) from one side of the room to another with a plastic spoon. Divide the players into two teams. The first person on each team uses a plastic spoon to transfer cotton balls from a full bucket on one side of the room to an empty bucket on the other side. Then they must run back to their team's line and hand the spoon to the next person on their team. If a cotton ball falls off the spoon and onto the floor, it must be left on the floor. At the end of the game, count the cotton balls in the buckets. The team with the most snowballs wins the race.

# Shabby Secret Santa or That Present Is Mine!

| | |
|---|---|
| About the game: | In Germany, people love *Schrottwichteln* at parties. |
| In the classroom: | A fun activity before the start of the holidays. |

| | |
|---|---|
| Number of players: | 10-15 |
| Equipment: | a dice; trashy Christmas presents, nicely wrapped |
| Duration: | 30 minutes |
| Preparation: | Each player wrapped a Christmas present. |

*How to play:*

This is variation of Secret Santa where people give away presents they received but don't actually want or exchange amusing, impractical or trashy gifts.

As with normal Secret Santa, a partner is drawn from among all participants in the group. Everyone writes their name on a piece of paper and puts it in a bag. With their eyes closed, each player draws a Secret Santa partner, but nobody reveals who they drew. Now a time period (usually a week) is set in which the gift is to be received. Ideally, your gift is something that you own, no longer need, is a little trash, and still suits your Secret Santa. Wrap it nicely, write the name of the person on it and give it away secretly.

*Variations:*

The way more exciting variant is rolling the dice, which makes the game more fun, it stays exciting until the end and it may be that the gifts find a completely unsuitable owner.

Each participant brings a wrapped gift to your Christmas party and places it in the middle of the table. The dice decide who gets which gift at the end. Each number on the dice represents a different rule:

On a 6:  The thrower can take a gift from the middle. Everyone only gets one gift when rolling the dice; the next 6 expires.
On a 1:  The player can unpack the gift.
On a 2:  The player swaps the chosen gift with that of another person.
On a 3:  All gifts are passed to the left.
On a 4:  All gifts are passed to the right.
On a 5:  Your left and right neighbours have to exchange gifts with each other.

The game ends when all players have unwrapped their gift or every player unwraps the gift in front of them when a predetermined time has passed.

*More Great Games Collections:*

Designs and Lines: Playground Marking Specialists, designsandlines.co.uk/blog/51-best-school-playground-games-for-kids

Ultimate Camp Resource, ultimatecampresource.com

Uplifter, www.uplifterinc.com/summer-camp-games-and-activities

Teambuilding.com, teambuilding.com

Twinkl, www.twinkl.com/

Verywell family, Active Play, www.verywellfamily.com/active-play-4157315

*About the Author:*

Geneviève Susemihl, PhD, has been a teacher and professor at schools and universities in Canada, the United States and Germany for almost thirty years. She is a sociologist and scholar in cultural studies and has published extensively on teaching methodologies, children's literature, heritage and other topics. She loves playing games and has applied many different games in classes and at home. Currently, she lives with her husband and her three children at the Baltic Coast in Germany.

Photo: Mathias Behrens